Spellcraft for Hedge Witches

Rae Beth is a practising hedge witch and a priestess of the Goddess. She writes acclaimed books on natural magic, from the viewpoint of green spirituality, and is regarded as an authority on the subject of solitary witch-craft. She aims to make hedge witchcraft more accessible to many, seeing the magic in life as every-one's birthright. Rae Beth also works as a psychic counsellor and is the author of the bestselling *Hedge Witch*, *The Hedge Witch's Way* and *Lamp of the Goddess*.

By the same author

Hedge Witch
Lamp of the Goddess (*formerly published as*
  Reincarnation and the Dark Goddess)
The Hedge Witch's Way
The Green Hedge Witch

Spellcraft for Hedge Witches

A Guide to Healing Our Lives

RAE BETH

Illustrated by Poppy Palin

ROBERT HALE

First published in 2004 by
Robert Hale, an imprint of
The Crowood Press Ltd
Ramsbury, Marlborough
Wiltshire SN8 2HR

www.crowood.com

www.halebooks.com

Paperback edition 2008

This impression 2017

© Rae Beth 2004

British Library Cataloguing-in-Publication Data
A catalogue record for this book is available from the British Library.

ISBN 978 0 7090 8618 5

Typeset by Derek Doyle & Associates, Shaw Heath
Printed and bound in Great Britain by CPI Group Ltd

This book is dedicated to the friends who have wisely and lovingly helped me through many a crisis. In particular: Sheila Broun, Helen Elwes, Joan Glyn, Helen Knibb, Harry Knibb, Dave Lister, Jan Nesbit, Poppy Palin, Paul Podworski and June Williams.

And to John Hale.

Contents

List of Spells

Please read the entire chapter containing each spell that interests you, as well as the early chapters on the formalities of magical procedure. Unless you are experienced in magic, the instructions may not be quite clear if read out of context.

Author's Note

Most of the herbs recommended in this book are in common use. They are regularly used either as herbal teas, tinctures, aromatherapy oils, incenses, ingredients in cosmetics or even as foods. However, if you have any medical problems such as high blood pressure, or if you are pregnant, it is up to you to discover whether there are any contra-indications for any particular substance. This applies to herbs you inhale (as incense smoke or vapourized oils) as well as to any you ingest.

Some of the herbs listed at the end of this book, such as mistletoe, are poisonous. Such plants may be carried as talismans or the wood made into wands or other magical objects. Others, like celandine, are narcotic. Obviously, they should not be drunk as teas or eaten, except on the advice of a qualified health-care practitioner.

Introduction

This is a book about spells which heal our lives. It is a self-help book (for anyone, not just for hedge witches), but with a difference. Whereas many such books encourage us to change *ourselves*, in the hope of thereby alleviating our problems, witchcraft has often had an unashamed bias towards dealing with the problem – or its perpetrator. Thus, we have old traditions of practices like working to return an ill-wish to the sender or of banishing troublesome spirits who may cause disease, ill luck etc. To twenty-first century readers, this may strike a medieval note, but I hope to present these old ideas in forms which can make sense for us now, in terms of present-day understanding, and without the superstition and, worse, scapegoating of others which can accompany such practices. I have also included spells of healing and self-transformation, to maintain a balance.

Above all, I hope that this book can teach an ethical *process*, a way of casting good spells for any purpose. The ideas within it can be endlessly adapted. But what is presented here is not the only way to do magic; it is just one way. However, it is tried and tested, and it is effective – at least for those who undertake it wholeheartedly.

Life, as my son once philosophically said, is 'not all Turkish delight and bouncy castles'. Crisis and difficulty are a part of it, for us all – things like divorce, bereavement, illness, job loss, depression. At such times, we need spells which deal with the possible causes of unhappiness or which bring a healing. But apart from the pain caused by these events (which is bad enough) the suffering can be compounded by human pettiness and many forms of abuse. It is sometimes even caused by them. Much of this may be our own responsibility, but not all. Either way, dark times are always an opportunity for new learning, for increases in wisdom and compassion that, ideally, grow as much as our own power does. That is, to my mind, the right goal for anyone, and, most especially, for those who practise magic.

I hope that this book will bring much healing.

Bright Blessings

Rae Beth

West of England

2004

1 The Purposes and Place of Natural Magic

There is magic within the universe that heals all ills. And there are spells for resolving any and every problem. This is an optimistic point of view, you might say, in what can be a most unhappy world! But I believe it and try to live by it, and so I practise hedge witchcraft.

When I say I work as a hedge witch, I mean I am of the solitary kind who works magic alone. I do not operate within a group or coven but generally cast spells on my own, as village wisewomen (and wisemen) have always done. The old-time village wisewoman is my role model. I am a fay, a kind of enchantress who practises nature magic, assisted by faeries. There are many of us around and we go by rather a lot of names – hedge witches, cunning men, wild, village or solitary witches, hedge wizards or fays – but we all practise natural magic and we do so alone, or (now and then) with friends or family. We do it for healing or inspirational purposes, for ourselves or others, for animals or places or the community.

But hedge witchcraft is not only for 'professionals'; it is for anyone. (By 'professionals', I do not mean people who are paid for casting spells – these days, very few people do that. I mean someone who has a commitment to natural magic as a life's work.) You do not have to be an actual witch to use natural magic for healing purposes during a life crisis. After all, you do not have to be a full-time writer to gain therapeutic benefit from keeping a journal. And you do not have to be a musician to sing a song.

Perhaps you already are a genuine witch or sense that you might want to become one. In that case, you will take the practices in this book a great deal further than those who would just like to glean helpful ideas. But if I had to answer the question, 'To whom does hedge witchcraft belong?', I would have to say, 'It belongs to and serves us all. It is for everyone.' In cultures less alienated from nature than our own present-day, mainstream one, many people have shared a magical worldview, whether or not they were the tribe's or community's shaman or wisewoman. This was so in remote parts of Britain as recently as the nineteenth century, when wandering folklorists like Alexander Carmichael and W.Y. Evans-Wentz found that people in country districts still used spells to make their households run more smoothly, or believed in faeries and strove to be on good terms with them. Magic is everyone's birthright. It is for us all.

Of course, it may be argued that an interest in magic is a regression to childlike beliefs and to superstition. But now that quantum physics and research into the paranormal by some scientists are beginning actually to prove the existence of psychic and magical laws, that argument is wearing rather thin. (For a comprehensive account of this, try reading Serena Roney-Dougal's classic *Where Science and Magic Meet*.) It would be more true to say that the superstitious have a naïve, fundamentalist approach to magic, rather than that magical belief is, in itself, naïve.

Others may wonder whether a practice as gentle as hedge witchcraft, which I have often described as 'an enacted nature poetry', can really yield any dramatic results. Do such spells have teeth and claws? Or the strength of a faery godmother? Or even, sometimes, the sly crackle of humour of a wise dwarf? Can they really bring change?

That is up to you, the practitioner, but if your desire to achieve your magical goals is genuine, then the answer to each of these is 'yes'. Natural magic really can heal shattered lives. It is better known as a means to try to procure what we want – a new lover, a better job or improved finances – and it does indeed work for such purposes. But this is not its most important remit. In the days when the old shamanic practitioner, village wisewomen and wizards, served their communities as psychic healers and counsellors, their work involved things like restoring the strength of a person's soul, banishing the effects of ill-wishes, connecting a person with the right healing spirits to cure their ailment and helping someone to renew their individual sense of purpose. These things helped rebuild damaged lives and restore continuity after a loss, because they spoke to our psychic needs in language our souls could understand. This was the real business of natural magic and it still is. Of course, it was also used to bless the crops and ensure a good harvest, and for many other matters concerned with the tribe's survival on a practical basis, but that was because it dealt in right relationship with spirit powers, to create harmony. Since then, it has often degenerated into a technique used to get what we want or to get even, in much the same way as poetry can degenerate into an advertising jingle or a slogan used for corrupt purposes. But that does not alter the sacredness of real poetry or real natural magic.

Hedge witchcraft can actually be at one with the self-repairing body of life, with that power that can bring evolutionary change out of disaster, as well as healing a disturbed equilibrium. Magic can do this because, at heart, all life is magical.

You will be wondering exactly what the skills and practices used in natural magic to achieve these ends are. They would require a lifetime's study for a person aiming to become a real expert. And they do take time, effort and patience. While genuine results can be obtained by a beginner, in no sense is witchcraft a 'quick fix' – but nothing is that produces results that are worthwhile and durable. It is rather like cookery or music. You would expect to learn to boil an egg or to sing your favourite song quite easily, and to advance beyond that would not be difficult. However, you would not expect to become an accomplished chef or musician unless you had studied and practised for many years.

Hedge witchcraft does not require complex, expensive equipment or special premises (like a cottage deep in a wild forest.) A few bowls and candles and a handful of herbs or a stone or feather or a bit of spring water may be all that you need – these, and some time alone. In Britain, a lot of our staples are hedgerow plants, like hawthorn, apple, elder or wild rose. But we also use plants from other lands and garden herbs, like rosemary, lavender and thyme. In other parts of the world, hedge witches may use the plants of their own locality or import others from our European tradition. But wherever we are, we work with the subtle, magical side of nature.

In the past, village wisewomen and cunning men some-times had an understanding of the medical aspects of plants. Nowadays, we leave that to qualified medical herbalists. It is never wise to prescribe any medicinal herbs for ourselves or others (except at a first-aid level) unless trained to do so. Therefore, we concentrate on what we are good at, weaving our healing spells, using plants and other things as talismans to amplify our psychic activity and to invoke the assistance of nature spirits. Speaking for myself and others like me, this means we do not ingest anything unless it is a well-known drink, like the herbal teas anyone might use for a cough or other minor ailment. However, we do make use of herbal incenses and vapourized essential oils. (Incenses are not essential, however. If you have chronic asthma or other medical reasons to avoid them, then you can cast spells in other ways.)

How does all this work? There is a very old body of knowledge, handed down through the generations, called 'magical correspondences', which can tell us which plants are known to be effective for which magical purposes. There are many excellent books on this subject and, at the end of this one, I include a list of my own. But in fact, if you think like a poet, you can work much of it out for yourself.

The rose, for example, corresponds to the magical vibration of love. The poet Burns said it and most Valentine cards make much of it! Everyone knows. You may also easily work out that things like strawberry jam and cream can be used in spells for the good life (to have 'jam and cream on both sides' as they say). Yew trees, so often found in graveyards, are symbolic of resurrection. Pungent herbs like rosemary and pine bring psychic as well as physical cleansing. There are, of course, more obscure meanings for less well known plants. But if you start to think about this, you can see that magical correspondences often depend on the symbolic associations or physical attributes of the plant concerned. Thus the yew is connected with resurrection because it regenerates itself when it dies, producing a new shoot from its own 'dead body'. Rosemary and juniper are psychic cleansers because they have antiseptic properties. (They have been used to fumigate sickrooms in the past.)

As well as a poetic understanding of nature's symbolism, we need other skills with which to cast spells. One of these is enchantment, the use of word magic. In fact, this is vital. The charm muttered over the steaming cauldron or (these days, more likely) the essential oil burner or herbal tea, is the main means by which we focus and direct our own psychic energy and, of course, communicate with the plant, elemental and faery spirits with whom we work. Enchantment is magical poetry in action. But you do not need to be a poet to use it! Plain doggerel verse will do. As long as it says what you mean and is said with conviction, it is good enough. Ideally, though, it should rhyme. It is said that the faeries, those traditional allies and teachers of witches, prefer a rhyme because it makes the magic more powerful. However, non-rhyming verse will often do.

The third key practice is ritual. Through actions that are ritualistic, we not only connect with the trans-logical realm of the spirits (by which I mean nature spirits, faeries, elementals and kindly helpful ancestral spirits and spirits of particular places), but also create a psychic pattern or template for what we want. An example of this could be something very easy, like sniffing a flower, to strengthen our own links with the magic of nature.

If the action is prefaced by words like the following, then an actual spell is cast:

As I breathe in the scent of a flower
so may I receive a witch's power.

It is said to be most effective to recite any brief spell three or (for even greater power) nine times. And, if the flower chosen for the spell above is elder (much associated with witches), ivy (linked with magical consciousness), or vervain, primrose, apple or willow (to do with the powers of enchantment), so much the better. But any flower not known for its malign tendencies, such as deadly nightshade or henbane, would do.

In fact, the spell described above contains all three key practices:

1 the use of magical correspondence (the flower corresponds to the magic of nature in general or to witchcraft/enchantment in paticular)

2 enchantment (the simple rhyme outlining your intention, explaining your goal)

3 ritual action (inhaling the flower's scent)

In order to understand how such fey techniques could actually be helpful in healing a life, we need to look at the witch's worldview, her or his understanding of why magic links with daily life. This consists largely of the idea that any action can have a psychic as well as a physical effect upon the web of life, especially if accompanied by the thought and the desire that it should do so. By using skills like enchantment, ritual and magical correspondence, all witches do is to heighten and intensify this fact. As we think, so we act. And as we act, we shape the psychic patterns of the future. We live in a magical universe. We can work with this creatively or can ignore it. But it will still be a fact.

2 The Worldview of the Witch

All matter is energy in condensed form, say the scientists. The Pagan worldview, held by many of today's practitioners of natural magic, is somewhat similar. It is a vision of the entire universe as one enormous, living being of energy (which we call spirit or life force) in manifest form. The Earth, the Sun, the Moon and the furthest stars of the most distant galaxy are one system, one living energy body. As a Pagan, I call this the body of the Great Mother Goddess, creatrix of life, she whose various aspects can each manifest that energy in numberless individual forms. That universal energy is seen on Earth, for instance, as only Mother Earth can manifest it, producing mountain range, zebra and orchid with quite incredible nonchalance, tirelessly bountiful; producing us, with all our capacities both for mindless destructiveness and sublime art; producing things like baroque music, sand paintings, haiku, ritual, gardens, calligraphy, through us, Her children; producing the wisdom of whales and the compassion of dolphins, the speed of tigers, the viciousness of piranha fish and the grace of horses.

Each of these, from mountain range and fish to music and writing are forms of universal spirit energy framed according to Mother Earth's particular potential. This basic 'spirit stuff' is sometimes called, by magical practitioners of many kinds, ether rather than Goddess, to make clear that this is but one aspect of the Creator Spirit, for we might as well also call the wind in the trees or the process of photosynthesis 'Goddess' (and indeed I do).

Scientists seem to be saying – or used to be saying – that all the energy in existence is in a concrete form. Magical folk believe that each entity has both a solid, manifest dimension and an underlying or indwelling etheric aspect – a psychic pattern. (Actually, in terms of quantum physics, science may now be saying much the same thing, but I must confess to knowing far less about these ideas than I should like to.)

Psychics can often *see* the etheric (or spirit-energy) dimension of a person, a creature, a tree or a place. This can appear as a shape of something that looks as though it is made of white mist – a human shape of white mist, if it is a person. Sounds familiar? It should, because this kind of thing is classically what people see when they psychically perceive a ghost. To a hedge witch (or anyone who takes the psychic aspect of life seriously), we each have a living ghost. And so does every creature, plant, hill, river and rock, and Earth Herself. Furthermore, our living ghosts are linked to the greater web of universal life, universal 'ghost'. By filaments of etheric energy (known to psychics as 'cords'), we connect with the land of our own locality and with the people, creatures and plants around us, who also link with others, and so on. The land, meanwhile, is linked by etheric filaments to the Sun, the Moon and other planets and stars. One entire system is one web of life, bearing and maintaining countless, countless individual forms. And because each individual life form dies and new ones are born (or old ones reborn) we can say that the spirit-energy of life always shifts shape, constantly mutating into one kind of body after another.

This white etheric substance, whether we see it as the billowing shape of a person, a creature or even a tree, can be of a living being or one who has died. It can cross the 'great divide'. It is 'between the worlds', as we witches say, and is only semi-physical. It is the most psychic substance that can be called manifest at all, and the first, coarsest thing we encounter in spirit realms.

As we all know, it is quite possible for a psychic to see the etheric shape of a departed human or animal. Indeed, we have a white, misty cat-shaped presence in our house, the ghost of a cat who once lived where we do now. Such friendly hauntings are quite common. An etheric presence can also be that of another order of being, a faery or some kind of local spirit associated with a special place, like a sacred hill or a stone circle. Frequently, such a spirit can be a place's guardian. At a holy well, it may take the form of a shining snake or eel, such as many psychic people have seen at Chalice Well in Glastonbury. But it often appears, at any holy well, as the white, misty 'ghost' of a woman.

Britain abounds in legends of these 'white ladies' as they are called. They are often thought to be connected to some piece of local history – a nun or a lady of the manor who died for love, for example. But actually, a white lady can be a spirit whose presence has been around for a lot longer than is suggested by local stories. From the point of view of a witch, she may be a faery, acting as the place's guardian, that is, looking after and maintaining the well's especially magical properties.

A ghost of a departed human or creature can be thin and wavering, sickly, bedraggled and lacklustre if the being concerned died of some wasting illness or is drained by unhappiness. In just the same way, our own living ghost can be weak or strong. If it is strong and healthy then, usually, so are we, since the body is a manifestation of the life pattern contained in the ghost. We each need our living ghost to be in good condition. We need a strong aura.

The aura, as seen by clairvoyants, is said to be ghost substance illumined by 'fire' or bio-electricity. It has the colours, textures and density created by our own moods and feelings, aims, aspirations and spiritual orientation.

But its state is also determined by how we live. If we tend to cut ourselves off from nature, our living ghost suffers. We need good food, adequate rest, sunlight, the Moon's magnetism, fresh air and water, and to walk freely upon the land (not tarmac) and connect with plants and fellow creatures. All these have etheric energy which will replenish ours (just as we share ours with others), and which we can absorb in a process as easy and automatic as breathing. Friends with a strong living ghost are a tonic. But people whose own energy is degraded by too much stress or by an unhealthy way of life can be a drain on us – as we can be upon others if we are not careful. Exhausted by stress or overwork, we can begin to take more etheric energy than we give, or give out energy which is uncomfortable for others.

This brings me to the point that etheric energy can be affected, moulded or directed, by our thoughts and feelings, in a constant interchange. But also, we can 'move the energy', as witches say, creating a template, a pattern, for future events, from the wave of etheric energy given off from our own bodies, having first drawn it in from inexhaustible sources like the wind, sunlight, seas and rivers and the land itself.

Witches can redirect or shape the pattern of energy that underlies events by the power of our thoughts and desires, expressed within a spell. This is the crux of witchcraft, the dictum that energy follows thought. But it follows it best when we begin relating to the dimension of 'living ghost', by working with subtle essences and spirit presences in an imaginative, ritualistic way. We can then create a new pattern, using our herbs, stones, symbols or whatever is appropriate, by associating them ritually with our chosen goal. This is often done by stating:

As [a symbolic action] occurs,
So [the desired aim] will happen.

'As this, so that', is the basic principle of sympathetic magic.

So witchcraft works on the borderline between psychic fact and poetic symbol. Therefore, the skill of enchantment is vital. For one thing, it expresses the intentions that shape the patterns of energy which underlie events. For another, it allows us to call upon spirits who can assist us, whether these be faery, nature spirits or elementals. In magical rhyme, which we call the chant or the spell, we 'spell it out' for the future we want.

In the end, it is the spirit that runs through all things, the Goddess Herself, who creates the original template for all life's themes. But sometimes, what She has given us is expressed in a distorted or negative way. This is when we, or other people, make the worst of things, missing our opportunities, responding poorly to challenges, undermining one another. Generally speaking, the job of a witch is to mend an etheric pattern, an underlying frame, so as to make the best of things, to heal our fate. The results can mend damaged lives, restore health and bring back a sense of purpose and meaning.

When it comes to moving the energy (changing the pattern of the future's ghost) by thought and imagination, popular techniques like creative visualization and affirmation can do it. Indeed, these can be an important part of a witch's repertoire; they are aspects of witchcraft by another name. But the use of natural objects to reinforce our theme and connect us with helpful nature spirits, and of ritual and enchantment, increase the effect many times. They provide very strong connections between the world of our thoughts and the world of events. Thus, we are not only thinking about or imagining changing a pattern of fate, we are enacting this symbolically and speaking it, while aligning ourselves with spirits of nature who correspond with the result we want. This gives a much stronger result.

Ether is the stuff of which all that we call 'supernatural' is made – or at least, on which it is based. It is the material of faeries, revenants, visions, apparitions, elemental and nature spirits and our own living ghosts. It conducts electricity and light, which is why, when faeries are seen, people often report them as shimmering or glowing, as silvery-white light or else radiant colours.

Actually, the term 'ether', as applied to psychic matters, is not an ancient one. In the sense in which I am using it here, it was popular with nineteenth-century occultists. Our forerunners in hedge witchcraft, the wisewomen and cunning men of the remote past, are unlikely ever to have heard it. When referring to ether, they might have said 'spirit' or 'spirit power' or called it by some name now lost to us. Words like 'glim' or 'glimmer' feel right to me, but whether this is a psychic retrieval of an old term or just a wild guess, I do not know.

In purely psychic realms, the dimension of faeries, ghostly phenomena and the like, where matter is largely composed of ether, changes in shape, colour and circumstance are very much swifter than they are in our own material world. That is why faeries are renowned as shapeshifters. In our slower realm, the ether or 'ghost material' can still be changed very quickly – all in the twinkling of a wand, as it were – but the manifestation of the new pattern in life takes a lot longer. Sadly, it is only in Harry Potter films that you just go 'ding' with your wand and achieve the desired result instantaneously. It is very rare to achieve a result at once. In natural magic, changes brought on by your spells most often occur at a natural pace.

You may be wondering where these etheric patterns go after witches have made them. Once they are created, do they just hover somewhere in your living room, or on a hilltop or wherever you cast your spell? In fact, they go straight to wherever they need to be, to fulfil their purpose. This does not mean that they fly off somewhere, like ghostly spaceships in deep space. Instead, there is a ripple effect, spreading on from the pattern, all the way to the place and time where the spell's goal can be achieved. It is rather like a wave in the sea. For a wave is not really a moving body of water, it just looks like one. Rather, a wave effect moves forward through the sea, lifting all the water through which it passes. So it is with an etheric pattern, until it 'breaks' like a wave on the shore, but in the form of an actual event.

This chapter has been nothing more than an attempt to explain some of the theory behind natural magic – a stumbling attempt, because these things partake of mystery and can never be entirely reduced to tidy concepts. When it comes to spirit power, it is only within our own spirits that we can understand what is happening. And the spirit speaks a language of symbol and metaphor. So, if you do not find these ideas about 'living ghost' and 'etheric webs' believable in a literal sense, treat them as poetic images of something that links the realms of magic with actual existence. You will find you get results just the same.

3 The Heal-anything Spell

After all that theory, I shall describe some hedge witchcraft in action. And since, as I said, this book is designed to deal with what I believe to be the real business of natural magic, the healing of wounded lives, I shall begin with an all-purpose healing spell.

If I had to pick just one very simple spell that would be most likely to heal any damage at all, whether mental, emotional, physical or spiritual, to mend any wounded life, then I would pick something like this one. It can be done during any crisis and in any kind of trouble. If your problem is not too difficult to resolve, then this may be all you need to do. For more deeply rooted or intractable problems, it is a valuable first resort but other, more specific, spells can be done on other occasions – as I shall describe in later chapters.

Actually, the process of looking for just the right magic, experimenting perhaps with many spells, and aquiring knowledge along the way, can constitute a healing journey. The fact of being involved in a magical *quest* for your cure can be an important part of the medicine. And, as a basis or a beginning for such a journey, the Heal-anything Spell is one good idea. But, I repeat, if your present problem is not difficult then something like this may be sufficient.

The Spell to Heal Anything

Fill a bowl with some leaves, twigs, flowers or berries
from an elder tree, or with a mixture, depending upon
which are available. Alternatively, you can buy dried
elderflowers from any good herbal supplier, if there are
no trees near to where you live. Fill a flask or bottle with
elder tea, wine or cordial from elderflowers or elderber-
ries, according to the season and your taste. Take these
with you and climb a grassy hill in a peaceful and rural
area, a place where you can be reasonably sure of being
uninterrupted by tourists, dog-walkers etc. If you can
think of no suitable hill nearby, then you might choose a
woodland clearing, an empty field or (if you can find one)
a deserted beach.

If you cannot manage to go anywhere like that because
of your health or transport problems, you can work at
home instead. Take a very long length of green string or
thread and arrange it in a rough circle on your floor to
mark out the area in which you will cast your spell. Unplug
the phone and work by candlelight. Play suitable back-
ground music (harp music, perhaps, or anything soft and
classical) to block out distracting noises.

Relax. Spend some time getting used to the ambience. If
you are on a hilltop, look all around you, at what you can
see in the distance. And what can you hear? What do each
of your five senses tell you right now? And your sixth
sense? Whether indoors or out, work out (with a compass
or by the sun) where east, south, west and north are. Place
your drink and your bowl of herbs at north. Stand facing
north and say:

I am here to cast a spell of healing, for myself.
I am here to be well.

Imagine a shining sphere of blue light surrounding the

area in which you are working, enclosing you. This is protective, because it symbolizes the blue atmosphere around Mother Earth. It is just outside and abutting on to your green thread circle, if you have one. And this, too, is psychically protective, denoting the green circle of nature as well as the helpful powers of faery, which are traditionally allied with witchcraft. (I shall go more fully into the need for psychic protection and the measures which provide it, later in the book.)

Remind yourself that you, too, are a part of nature – a nature spirit in human form – magical, capable of mediating faery powers as a tree or a creature can, and just as full of mysterious potential as any other of Earth's psychic phenomena. Align yourself for a moment with these, outside the safe margins, with elves and weird ones and angels disguised as beggars and wild woods and moontides. These are not threatening to you as they are to the more convential humans, for they are within a realm that is yours as well – the realm of magic. Inside you, is something as darkly bright and full of power.

Say:

I call on the elemental spirits, the free and the wild,
Those of wind, flame, pool, stone and ether,
To see that my spell is woven well.
Let this be, in the names of the Mother of Life
And of the Green God, nature's guardian,
Whom I invoke as Love and Wisdom,
For I am Their untamed child.

Go to the centre of your circle and spin round nine times, deosil (clockwise) chanting as you go:

Now let the spirit of elder tree
bring all the help that I need to me.

Deosil, known as the way of the sun, is the direction associated with spells of increase, renewal and growth. The
other direction, widdershins (or counter-clockwise, the way
of the moon) is used in dances for spells of decrease or
banishing, for example to banish poverty or loneliness,
rather than to invoke prosperity or love. It is also used, ritually, as an action that takes you within, to the place of
personal and psychological transformation, dreams and
trance journeys.

If you find turning round nine times very difficult or
impossible, then you can visualize doing so. But do not
picture *yourself* turning deosil. Instead, picture the *landscape* spinning past you as you turn round. Be right within
the visualization, not somewhere outside it, observing yourself. To help this process along, imagine yourself upon a
green hill. Now look down at your own feet. They should be
in the same perspective as when you look at them physically. Visualize stretching out your arms in front of you. Do
they look more or less as they would if you did this with your
body? If so, you are visualizing correctly. If not, or if you
have difficulty with any visualization, and therefore cannot
see anything much, simply say:

In my soul, I am on a green hill, where I turn
Deosil, nine times. As I go round, I say,
'Now shall the spirit of elder tree
Bring all the help that I need to me.'

Witchcraft is practical. We adapt practices and techniques to our particular needs and circumstances. In this
way, we can achieve results wherever and however we
are. Even the smallest and simplest magical practice can
be enough to restore our balance or to make improve-
ments. A feather upon the scales may be enough. If it is
not, it will at least push things in the right direction,
making a more thoroughgoing and physically enacted

spell more possible in the future. So do not worry if even visualization is beyond you. Just state what would be happening if you could do the spell fully. And imagine it as much as you can. (Paradoxically, for the really experienced, visualization of the type we call trance-work or path-working can change a life as much as an enacted spell would do.)

At the conclusion of your deosil spin or your visualization, put your hands in the bowl of elder and pour etheric energy into the contents. Imagine that the elder is being imbued with your ghost power. Imagine this and it will be so.

Then place a handful of whatever is in the bowl on the ground at the east of your circle. Place more handfuls at the south, west and north and, finally, a big one at the centre. Face north again and say:

> *The universe holds the right cure for every ill.*
> *I stand and draw towards me what I most need.*
> *I do this by the power of my own will*
> *And by elemental spirits and elder tree.*
> *And as I summon, beckon, call,*
> *With harm to none, I shall draw all*
> *I need of well-being. So May It Be.*

Now face east and say: 'Come, cure, here.' Extend your arms slowly in front of you, palms upward. Curl your fingers towards you, in a beckoning gesture and then draw them in, slowly, to touch your heart.

Move round the circle deosil and stand facing south. Repeat, 'Come, cure, here,' and make the beckoning gesture.

Move round to the west and repeat the words and gesture, and again at the north. Then return to face east. Your progress should have traced out a small circle. Go to the centre and repeat again, 'Come, cure, here.'

Turn deosil in a complete circle, your arms extended in the beckoning position. Bring your fingertips in to touch your heart one last time.

Go to the north of your circle and take the lid off your drink. If you have brought a chalice, wine glass or mug, now is the moment to use it. Place your hand over the full receptacle and say:

The elder's power is strong and sure.
I drink and am at one with her.
And so with what shall bring my cure.

Now drink, savouring the moment.

When you are ready, put down the chalice. Sit more comfortably or lie down. Close your eyes and visualize the shining web of living ghost that links all things. Or, if you cannot visualize, mentally tell yourself about it. Just as veins and capillaries take blood around the body, feeding the right nutrients to every cell, so this system brings the life-giving ether, the primary substance, that sustains existence, to every place and plant and creature. Feel yourself, by the power of the elder, drawing towards you the cure that you need for whatever ails you. These come along the shining pathways, perhaps from more than one direction, towards your heart to circulate throughout your whole being. The shining pathways are, in fact, an aspect of the whole living ghost of all Creation. They are also, at the same time, the web of fate, which will now bring the right answer. Into your life will come the best medicine if you are ill, or good advice from a doctor or health practitioner; or a new lover or circle of friends if you are lonely; or a new way of life if you need that; or help and support in dealing with some abuse; or whatever you need for well-being.

After concluding this visualization (or description), say, 'It is done. All is well.'

Then stand and face north and say:

I thank you, Lady and Lord –
Great Goddess and God –
For your blessing upon my spell.
I thank you, spirits of wind and flame
And pool and stone and ether, for all is well.
And I thank you, spirit of elder.

Now visualize or describe a protective sphere of blue light around yourself rather than around your circle. This is to enable you to re-enter the everyday world without being badly affected by its harshness. Casting a spell can leave you in a very sensitive state. You may not realize this while doing the work, but your psychic senses may become attuned to nuance and atmosphere in a way that is subtle but very immediate, rather like coming back from a fortnight in faeryland or a year on distant and largely uninhabited island.

Afterwards, if you have been working indoors, sweep or pick up the elder from the floor and put it in a bag, ready to be returned to a hedgerow, or a wood, or a canal bank or anywhere else that is suitable. If you have used elder-berries indoors, then you may regret it, as they will stain the floor, if trodden on. And it is not wise to put the berries on your garden unless you want elder trees to grow there.

If you wonder about the spell's efficacy, consider this. At the level of quantum physics, Creation really is a self-restoring, self-regulating system. Out there, somewhere, is what you need to restore you to health and happiness. Perhaps it is a particular herbal remedy or homoeopathic prescription, the loving support of like-minded people, water from a holy well, a new opportunity to earn some money, a new place to live, the chance to see a hospital consultant, or a change of attitude brought about by the right book or chance encounter.

The universe is one Being, of which we are each a cell in the one great body. Within this entirety, there exists what we each need. And we do not need to have the least idea of what this remedy might be when doing the spell, because the elder tree knows.

Why the elder tree? Why do we work with this particu-lar plant? In folklore, the spirit of the elder is believed to be a witch or a faery. Symbolically, she can represent the Goddess of nature's healing powers in Her aspect of regeneration. This may be why flints shaped like elder leaves have been found in ancient longbarrows. The elder has marvellous powers of rebirth, a theme our ancestors may have been keen to emphasize when burying their dead. When cut down, it grows back with almost miraculous tenacity – or a demonic tenacity if you're trying to eradicate it from your garden! But perhaps it is better not to do that without transplanting it or replanting another elder in some other place. There is an old saying about it, which goes like this:

Elder is the Lady's tree.
Cut it down and cursed you'll be.

It suggests that this particular tree may once have been held very sacred indeed. (The Celts imposed the death penalty on people who cut down trees that were sacred to deities. So far as I know, they did not regard the elder as one of these, but perhaps for the earliest inhabitants of these islands, it was.)

Whichever way you look at it, the elder is not only connected with ancient beliefs and linked with the faeries; it is also a prime symbol of renewal. It is about growing back, recovery. Tradition also had it that the elder could cure all the ills that beset humanity – an enigmatic statement.

A word here about the Mother of Life and the Green God, in whose names the spell is cast. In fact, the Goddesses and Gods whom witches worship are various aspects of the life force, the great creative power that keeps life in being. Most of us feel that this power has both a female and a male expression. You might prefer to call them 'Creatrix and Creator', or by deity names which are particularly meaningful to you. The reason for working in Their names at all, is that if we consider our spell-casting as a sacred process, then we are more likely to be mindful of the need to weave magic with care, in accordance with the highest principles. Moreover, such spells receive the blessing of beneficent and loving deities.

Some may argue that the life force does not always seem beneficent and loving, that in fact it can be cruel and ruthless. That is so. But most witches trust that the overall trend of life is towards order and harmony, and that every kind of disaster can be an opportunity for fruitful change and increased wisdom. We are optimistic enough to believe that Earth Herself has a wise and creative spirit and is actually divine. Many of us feel that a lot of human problems are caused by a lack of trust in the cycles of life, wherein every death or loss is always followed by some kind of rebirth, as nature demonstrates.

Ideally, the Heal-anything Spell should be done in spring or early summer, upon the tide of nature's revival and growth, when fresh, flourishing life returns to the woods and fields. At need, it can be done any time of the year but preferably when the moon is waxing.

4 The Hedge Witch's Temple

Where are the broomsticks and cauldrons? Where are the magic wands and candle-lit altars? Are they not used in hedge witchcraft? Yes, they are. But as practitioners of natural magic, we must first come into a psychic relationship with the land and the whole web of life. We can then take our cauldrons and other equipment outside with us to fields and woodlands, if that is what we wish. Or we can work indoors, which may bring the advantage of greater freedom from interruption. The choice is yours. It is usually easier for those starting out on the path of natural magic to work with some degree of formality, as this brings confidence. So I shall now describe a more formal style and the tools it requires.

Those who are experienced in magic might want to skip some of the following, as it will cover themes that are familiar from their work and are found in many other books, including my own previous ones. However, you may also find that the next few chapters will put some old ideas in a fresh context.

Choose a circular area in a quiet room. This may mean moving a few pieces of furniture to clear a space, but you do not need an enormous circle. Just do the best that you can. Make sure that the phone is unplugged and that you will not be disturbed. You can mark out your circle with string or a coil of rope, or draw one with chalk, or put down a round mat, or just, as most of us do, imagine a circle. It need only be a rough circle – geometrical precision is not necessary.

A circular space is used because it symbolizes nature's cycle of birth, growth, maturity, death and rebirth – the round of existence in which we all partake. This is most clearly shown by the cycle of seasons, where spring, the year's birth, is followed by summer, autumn, winter and then the next spring, showing (in vegetation and in the life of creatures), a sequence of youth, growth, fruition, decay and new birth.

Hedge witches tend to believe that this pattern extends to all life, to all that exists, though it may not play itself through annually. (The human life cycle, all the way round from birth to growth to maturation to death and then rebirth in a new body may take a very long time indeed.) So, when working magic, we temporarily dedicate a circular space to our purposes, in order to state that we stand within the larger pattern of all Creation, and align ourselves with that. Thus, though we do not have special buildings or temples, for our natural magic, we can take our idea of a temple wherever we go.

This spiritual orientation – standing within the circle of all Creation – helps us remember a spell's widest implications. Anything that helps or heals any one of us helps us all, but a spell that harms anyone harms everyone. This is because, within the great circle of all life, we are all connected. The effects of what we do will always ripple out, affecting the people close to us and those close to them and so on, in a knock-on effect that is awesome to think about. Indeed, any one of us has massive power for good or ill, however seemingly insignificant our lives. When that is amplified by the practice of magic, we can tip the scales in respect of large-scale events and movements in ways we may never know. We stand within the circle of all Creation, affected by and affecting all that exists.

Each of the compass points of the circle, as well as the

centre, is associated with a particular aspect of Creation. In witchcraft, we name these elemental aspects as Air (east), Fire (south), Water (west), Earth (north) and Ether (centre). They are the materials out of which all forms of life are made, in the same way that each shade of every colour is made from one or more of the primary colours (red, yellow and blue), plus black and white.

Ether, as already discussed, is not quite like the other four elements. You cannot see or feel it unless you are psychic. But it is in all things everywhere. There is ether in fresh or salt water, earth, wind and fire, as well as in all the separate entities in all organic life – plants, creatures and places. There is much less in what is non-organic, except that the touch of human hands or the proximity of human or other creaturely activity may bestow more – e.g. upon a concrete wall or a plastic plant pot which are part of a garden. This is why cities can be such exhausting places, and why the typical suburban environment seems so lifeless. (Comparitively speaking, it *is* lifeless).

Place a small table at the north of your circle to serve as an altar. Upon it, arrange some fresh foliage (in winter, bare twigs), flanked by two candles. These bits of tree symbolize the mythical World Tree, which is found in so many Pagan traditions throughout the Earth, and around which all Creation is said to revolve. Also have a wand, a small bowl of water and a stone. These symbolize Air, Water and Earth respectively, while your candles denote Fire. You may also want to display a knife which you use only for spell-casting. The fact of having set it aside for magic makes it an 'athame', a witch's knife. There are formal ways of doing this 'setting aside', or consecration, but many people feel that simply keeping it upon your altar for a while, or mentally dedicating it to magic while holding it in your hands is effective enough. The athame comes in handy for things like the ritual cutting of a cord or for carving the bark from a slim piece of wood to make a wand. But it is not essential, in my view, to have it always upon your altar.

A cauldron or cooking pot should be placed at the circle's centre, if you have enough room for this to be practicable. If not, then you might put it under the altar, positioned beneath your symbolic World Tree. Or, depending upon the part it is to play in the rite (if any), upon the altar top with all your other things. The cauldron represents Ether, the spirit that runs through all things, because it suggests each one of the other four elements. (Fire is used to heat food in a cooking pot, water is in the pot with the food, solid Earth is represented by the ingredients and Air by steam rising.) Most importantly, it also symbolizes the womb of the Great Mother Goddess, who brings forth increasingly subtle and complex life forms from primordial beginnings, rather as cooking transforms raw materials. So the cauldron means constructive change and creative alchemy. For these reasons, it is one of the prime symbols of natural magic.

Just like the words used in poetry, ritual tools in natural magic have many layers of symbolic meaning. But then, hedge witchcraft is a process of enacted nature poetry.

Now for the witch's broom. This can be used, ritually, to sweep your magic circle clean of its everyday atmosphere and of any destructive psychic energy before beginning a rite. By destructive energy I mean any psychic charge left over from an argument or something like a bad mood or depression. Such things can fill a room with what you might call tainted ether, etheric energy soured by unhappiness, which creates a bad atmosphere. This becomes an unintended lure for passing spirits of ill intention (and such beings certainly do exist), who feed on negative energy and grow fat on it and then stay around, making trouble. Sweeping the magic circle is a ritual act to disperse them. Some people swish the broom through the air as well as over the floor when doing this, on the basis that bad energy does not all sink down to floor level! Experiment and see what feels right to you. (If you cannot be bothered with it at all because it feels rather like 'magical house-work', then you can burn incense or vaporize a psychically cleansing essential oil instead.) The magic broom has uses other than purification and is especially linked with 'flying' or trance journeys, but that is a completely different subject.

Traditionally, the twigs of a witch's broom should be of birch. This is because that tree is said to have the magical property of dispelling wickedness and negativity. In the past, babies' cradles were often made of birchwood to protect the new-born infant from wicked spirits or malicious thoughts. More sinisterly, birch rods were used to beat criminals, because it was thought that this would drive out demons or expel the person's own badness. Actually, however, birch trees are gentle and beautiful; their spirits are not a bit punitive. Instead, from a magical point of view, they have a freshness and grace that seems to disperse any malice or psychic squalor by the assertion of something that stands above such things, untouchable. (What the birch spirit can stand for exactly is an innocent incorruptability that is at one with certain kinds of faery, a spirit that is both ethereal and unconstrained, wild. Next time you look at a birch tree, see if that feels like the right description to you.)

If you do not have a birch-twig broom, then you can ritually brush around the circle with a handful of birch twigs – assuming that there is a birch tree nearby, from which you can collect some.

Such are the basic tools of magic. The most important is probably the cauldron, or a bowl that can stand in for one. If I had to pick the most useful of all equipment for any hedge witch, I should probably decide on a set of bowls of varying sizes. You do not need to keep them on an altar all at once. But you would be surprised how often you need a receptacle for herbs, liquids, a cord, special stones or offerings for familiar spirits, or any one of a host of other things. In practice, the objects any hedge witch will choose to place upon an altar will reflect their individual style to some extent. Some may find it extremely important always to display a cauldron or chalice prominently.

Many others will feel it is not complete without a collection of bird feathers, fossils, stones, shells and ornaments depicting plants or creatures.

Begin with the basics and see, gradually, what you want to add as your style develops.

When casting spells, it can help to wear clothes that you

have set aside for the purpose. You may want to become creative about this and make or buy a robe, cloak or shawl that depicts the most magical aspect of yourself. Do you see faery presences in wild countryside? Or feel akin to the faery Otherworld in your soul? Wear bright red or green, which are said to be colours especially favoured by faeries. Perhaps you may want to emphasize your links with nature, the Earth. Wear brown or a combination of brown and green. Does the hidden side of life call to you, the ancient mysteries of life, death and rebirth? Then black might be your choice. These are just obvious ideas. You may think of something entirely different that is more meaningful to you. And that will be your right choice because there is certainly no uniform in hedge witchcraft and no dogma. (There is also a strong case to be made for wearing just what you wear all the time, nothing unusual, because this is a statement that magic is everywhere and always present. It closes the gap between magical otherworldliness and everyday life. However, this is a stance that you might find easier to hold when you are more experienced.) Whatever feels right to you *is* right.

These then are some of the main tools and concepts of natural magic. But to become reliant on equipment is to miss the point that magic is not just in specific items but in every aspect of life and in each of us. The experienced hedge witch can make do with a handful of leaves or a stone picked up from the path, for example, and with the word-spells that drift into our hearts and minds on the wind and from faery. These things are all that we really need in an ideal world. In the world as it is, having special tools for magic can help us when we feel low. They invoke magical power in us by association when we just look at them. When we feel far from faery-haunted or elemental places, they can remind us of and orientate us towards, such things. Besides, if we do not learn something of the more formal ideas, practices, symbols and tools of magic, it can be harder to work informally with real effectiveness. In natural magic, as in any art, rules and tools are not meant as a creative straitjacket. They are there to be broken at will, or dispensed with. However, you can best do this with safety and with style if you know what they are.

5 Casting a Magic Circle

When you have chosen an area for your circle, arranged an altar and placed upon it your magical tools, and swept the circle with your birch broom or else used some cleansing oils or incense, like rosemary or juniper, you will be ready to begin magic.

Stand at the north point of your circle and face your altar. The reason for doing this is said to be that the Earth's own power flows from that direction. However, there is a Mayan prophecy that, in the year 2008, there will be a 'polar shift', which means, so far as I know, that the biomagnetic power of the north will be in the south instead. Our compasses will point due south and we shall all need to face south in our circles if this turns out to be true. Meanwhile, we face north – and, I suppose, may continue to do so for symbolic reasons.

Say something like the following, and mentally direct your words towards the direction of spirit, the psychic realm.

I cast this circle in the names of the Mother of Life and of the Horned God, nature's guardian. May it be a meeting place of love and wisdom.

As ever, if you do not feel comfortable with the titles I have given the Creatrix and Creator, then choose your own. So long as you invoke your chosen One/s in an aspect of natural creativity, harmony and the wild magic that keeps all life in being, then you will be on the path of Paganism that upholds natural magic.

Pick up your wand and walk three times around the circle, deosil, visualizing that a flame of blue light is emanating from the wand's tip. Eventually you will be surrounded by this blue light, which has closed around your working area in a protective bubble. If you do not yet own a satisfactory wand, use a twig. In the absence of that, point a finger. The best woods for all-purpose wands are oak, ash, apple or birch. Apple is best for those whose work involves lots of contact with faery helpers, while the other three woods are suitable for most of us.

The point of the blue light is twofold. First, it is there to contain the power which you will shortly raise for magic, so that it does not just disperse before you have used it. Secondly, it confers some psychic protection. Try to visualize it surrounding your circle completely. See it as a blue sphere, like the blue atmosphere around Mother Earth, not just as a circular 'wall'. The same kind of blue sphere can quickly be visualized around yourself for personal psychic protection wherever you are, at need. If you are unable to visualize, just mentally state that it is there and it will be.

Psychic protection is always a good idea when you are in a psychically receptive state, such as when casting spells. I have never heard of anyone being possessed by an evil spirit and then turning violent as a result of natural magic done for a sensible objective; your own soul's integrity will be sufficient protection against that. Nothing can take over your whole being and make you its automaton on a psychic level, any more than a bad person can make you their spiritual slave, within the everyday world, unless you let them. Any person of normal goodwill and strength of spirit would be immune to that kind of thing, just by the virtue of their own nature. Nevertheless, you can be scared or depressed by the unpleasant atmosphere of a passing spirit, in much the same way that we can be exposed to problems from other people we pass in the street. Physically, in the everyday world in Britain, there is normally no serious danger if you are sensible and, for example, avoid dark alleyways at night. The magical equivalent is to avoid practising magic in any place where a tragic or violent event has recently taken place, especially if it is known to be haunted. In just the same way that you would forgo walking in some parts of town to avoid trouble, do not do magic in a haunted or negative atmosphere unless your are a skilled exorcist. The psychic and magical aspects of life are not merely psychological and there are spirits of all types.

Replace your wand upon the altar and then go round your circle to each of the compass points in turn, and finally to the centre.

At the east, say something like this:

I call upon the elemental spirits of Air, the breath of life, to watch over me and assist me with magic. Spirits of voice that sings and of wind that lifts wings, hail and welcome.

At the south say:

I call upon the elemental spirits of Fire, the flame of life, to watch over me and assist me with magic. Spirits of bright energy in each living being and in hearth fire and in Earth's core, hail and welcome.

At the west, say:

I call upon the elemental spirits of Water, the flow of life, to watch over me and assist me with magic. Spirits of dream seen reflected in fresh stream, spirits of deep feeling, hail and welcome.

At the north, say:

I call upon the elemental spirits of Earth, the body of life, to watch over me and assist me with magic. Spirits of stone and bone, flesh, vegetation, matter of fact, hail and welcome.

At the centre, say:

I call upon the elemental spirits of Ether, the wraith of life, to watch over me and assist me with magic. You who are everywhere, in all directions, in Fire and Water and Earth and Air, sustaining, I bid you hail and welcome.

There are many variations on this theme of calling in the elemental spirits, or guardians of the four quarters as they are sometimes known. But nowadays, almost everyone practising natural magic does it in some form or another. For the Heal-anything Spell, I suggested a rhyme in which the elemental spirits were referred to mainly by symbols, as wind, flame, pool, stone and ether. That calling in was informal. But it does not really matter *how* it is done; its purpose is spiritual orientation, enhanced psychic protection and, as the invocations suggest, the gaining of assistance with magic.

The whole of the natural world consists of these elements in varying combinations. For instance, a herb consists of Earth, (its solid materials), Water, Fire (the plant's bioelectric field) and Air (plants breathe, taking in carbon dioxide, giving out oxygen), and also Ether (the plant's spirit or etheric form). A flame is made only of Fire and Ether, a rainbow of Fire, Water and Ether, and animals of all five elements. Each of these elements, in magical theory, also has a particular aspect of life associated with it. Thus, thoughts, communication and movement are connected with Air, vitality, passion and creative will with Fire, feelings, dreams, poetic meaning, with Water, and physical matters with Earth. Ether can be concerned with anything at all, but especially with memories (collective or personal), past life matters, trance journeys, mediumistic experiences and contact with faeries. Certain matters, like health, can be within the domain of any of the elements or all of them. People make use of this by including something of a particular and appropriate element within a ritual practice. For example, many people are now reviving the traditional practice of asking a deity or a spirit of healing for help when they are ill. They do this by tying a prayer or a piece of ribbon, cloth or some other token to a tree, so that the wind may take their plea for healing to the spirit realms.

It becomes clear with experience that if we place ourselves within a circle that symbolizes all life, all Creation, and concern ourselves with the elements that are in all life forms, then the process of spell-casting is deepened and enhanced both psychically and spiritually. And we have magical help from the spirits of elemental powers, as well as from whichever nature or faery spirits we have invoked (for example, in the Heal-anything Spell, the elder tree spirit). As a hedge witch, you do not cast spells alone. You do not seek to reweave life's web single-handed, in spite of the fact that this is generally a solitary practice. For it is not a matter of pitting our wills against fate, nor of trying to dominate events by using magical clout. Instead, ideally, there is a process of coming into conjunction with elemental and nature spirits, with the blessing of divine powers, to tilt the balance of destiny in a creative, harmonious direction, to work with what *is* and to maximize best-case scenarios, at one with life. This takes a delicate balance between a wise acceptance of what fate decrees and an attempt to rewrite the future, according to our best dreams. From somewhere within the union of these two apparently irreconcilable opposites comes – at its best – hedge witchcraft. And it can be by standing symbolically within the circle of all Creation, together with elemental spirits and under the aegis of the divine, that we reach the state of consciousness, the spiritual orientation, that is required.

Life is a magical-spiritual-physical continuum, in which each individual spirit can express, via the elemental forces, some aspect of universal Spirit, or the divine. Therefore, having called in elemental helpers and defined the magical space in which we are working, the next step is to invoke divine presences. For a spell-casting must always be a sacred process if it is to be genuinely healing and not merely an attempt to steal a march on events. Here are some suggested invocations of the Mother and Father of Life. Say them or something like them, out loud or in your mind.

Prayer to the Goddess

Great Mother, you who are creative power in every cell of our bodies and in each star and in all the multitudes of plants and creatures, on land or under the sea, I call upon you to waken, within

*me, the power to cast healing spells. As vibrant Lady of Faery, bless
my work of magic. Make all things well. For you are the wisdom of
nature and deep enchantment and the pattern of harmony, throughout all worlds.*

Prayer to the God

*I call upon you, Great Horned God, the Father of Wildness within
each heart. Lead me, as I turn within to untamed faery places. You,
who are prompter of each step beyond the safe boundaries, let magic
start. But guide and watch over me now, as I hunt the moment
when power rises and spells are cast.*

Next, state the purpose of your work. Say something like:
'I am here to work magic for . . . [psychic protection,
justice, good fortune, or whatever you wish].'

There is only one thing left to do now, before your actual
spell-casting. It is, however, a big thing, so I will leave it for
the next chapter.

6 Raising the Power for Magic

We now come to a vital point, the question of how to raise power for magic. Without it, our rites of spell-casting will feel empty and theatrical, a mere recital of words and symbolic actions with only an abstract significance. People refer to the power by various names, like 'fire' or 'bioelectric energy'. Others point out that achieving an altered, more psychic state of consciousness is actually 'the power'. Both schools of thought are correct. And doubtless there are other factors as well. Magical power has as many factors as physical, mental, creative or any other kind of power. Myself, I think it helps to concentrate upon the etheric component, the 'fuel' and medium of all spell-casting. Then the other requirements will tend to take care of themselves.

For magic, we need a supply of etheric energy in excess of that which is in our own living bodies. It is this energy which forms the swirls and patterns of all created life, past present and future. It is this, also, which helps to give us the psychic and physical strength with which to cast spells. So we need plenty of it to strengthen ourselves, and we need an excess so that some can be moulded into the pattern of fate required, the psychic blueprint. Once the magical working has changed the etheric web, there will be a change within the everyday world. Your newly made picture of what will be, having an etheric reality, will ripple out, causing a change in the previous 'blueprint', the one that would have prevailed without your spell.

Energy follows thought as a rule. If we have enough of this wraith energy (etheric energy) within our bodies, then our thoughts will first mould it into a pattern of our own power, if we want that. Then up comes the inner fire, which, in the East they call *kundalini*, and we feel a surge of magical ability.

Etheric power is everywhere, in everything. It is in Air, Fire, Water and Earth, the constituents of life, and in all life forms. It carries what the Hindus call *prana*, and the Chinese *chi*. It appears to be what the Polynesians call *mana* and connect with the spirit of the moon and realm of the dead (i.e. ghosts). The Celts also sometimes referred to the spirit world of the dead as Emain, or Hy-Many, linking this idea of ghostly white 'moon forms' with spirit and magic.

Our own bodies and those of all creatures, plants and natural wild places give off a certain amount of Ether and also draw it in from our surroundings, as I have said. For the most part this process is self-regulating. Just as we can be warmed or chilled by external factors and also give out our own physical warmth, usually without having to think about it, so we take in and give out Ether, the power of the 'living ghost'. It is only when we are etherically depleted that we sense that there is something wrong. Then we need activities like gardening, walking in the country or visiting the sea to put us right. Lying on the earth in sunlight is excellent, too.

You may think that this whole involvement of the body with magic is a strange concept. Surely it is in our minds or our souls that magic is generated? Yes, that is certainly so. But Pagans tend to believe that mind, soul, spirit and body are not separate entities but different resonances of the same thing, of an individual being. Body, soul and spirit reflect and echo one another, while awareness, which we call 'mind', can travel between them. Thus, the whole self is implicated in anything that we do, anything that we are.

There are a variety of ways to raise etheric power but basically we run it through our own bodies, drawing it to us from other, inexhaustible sources and then directing it, by the powers of will, thought and enacted spell, into our magical work. This is the ethical way to cast spells. There is another way, ancient and immoral, which is to spill something's blood, to kill an animal or a bird, perhaps.

Blood holds a huge ammount of etheric and bioelectric energy; it conducts life. But to a modern hedge witch, blood-spilling is abhorrent because it means stealing energy from another being – stealing it so thoroughly that you take all they will ever have by murdering them. However, it must be said that our Pagan ancestors did not all see it that way. They reasoned that if you could kill an animal for food, then there was no reason why you should not also do so to increase magical power, especially if this would bring benefit to the crops and so to the entire community. Even human beings were sometimes offered up in this way for the sake of major magic designed to help the entire tribe.

This is, of course, shocking and repugnant to us. But before we throw up our hands in horror at the barbarism of past Pagan practices, we need to remember that very many lives have been sacrificed by non-Pagan nations, for the sake of empire-building and economic advantage, and it is still going on.

As a hedge witch and priestess of the Great Mother, I advocate a world in which no blood is spilt for magical or monetary purposes – ever. Ends do not justify means and, as a species, we need to grow beyond thinking that they do. The only exception that I would make to the rule that no blood sacrifice should ever be made is a woman's use of her own menstrual blood. This harms no one and is her own to use as she wills. I have myself used it, with excellent results. (It is done by annointing herbs, stone or other tokens, with blood, at an appropriate point in the rite.) The equivalent practice for a man would be to use sperm. However, natural magic does not depend upon such methods. They are short cuts to power but are not necessarily more 'advanced' merely because they break a taboo or challenge our perceptions about what is 'nice' behaviour. I mention them to illustrate the vast range of approaches to the subject of raising power.

Today's most popular methods take a little more effort, and involve drawing in an excess of energy from some completely unending source, like the night sky, the Earth Herself or the ocean or, as in the example which I shall give, from the elements. It is done, as when directing power outwards, by thought and statement or visualization. To make this more effective, you can chant a rhyme, calling upon vast stores of power. This not only serves your purpose but also changes your consciousness to a dreamier and more magical state. By its rhythm and repetitions, it lulls the everyday, rational mind, giving the intuition (the brain's right hemisphere perhaps) a chance to wake up, sense subtle forces and become psychically aware and active.

Many people like to dance or spin in a circle while chanting for power, since dancing is another time-honoured method of changing consciousness and raising energy. It is widely used in shamanic cultures and also in present-day Wicca. But you do not have to do this if ill-health or lack of space make it difficult. Instead, you can make use of the intense concentration which your stillness will permit – a more meditative approach. Experiment and see which works best for you if your circumstances are such that either is possible. The main thing is to raise etheric energy somehow. Pouring it into your work afterwards is the easy part, since energy follows thought and feeling quite automatically.

You do not need to see or visualize the etheric energy while you are casting your spell. You do not have to picture 'white ghost stuff' taking on the symbolic pattern of your spell's goal. All you need to think about, or to visualize or describe, is the spell's outcome. For example, if you are doing a self-healing, picture or describe your life as a fit person. Imagine or tell yourself about the feeling of vitality in your healthy body. If you do this, the etheric form will take care of itself, so long as there is enough Ether available, while you work.

Raising power is very much easier out of doors, where there is so much of the living ghost energy all around us, in nature. At places known to be sacred sites, like holy wells or special hills, there can be huge amounts of it, visible to the psychic as clouds of white mist at ground level (even on a sunny day). On the other hand, in a crowded area like southern Britain, you can be freer from interruptions indoors, unless you choose an unpopular time, like when it is dark or the weather is gloomy. An overcast day can be very useful; while everyone else is inside, you can be out there in your waterproof, getting on with the magic! This sounds extremely unglamourous, but it works. It is a very British approach, which probably sounds a bit insane to those from warmer, less populated places.

Indoors, you can decorate an altar with stones, fresh flowers, bowls of spring water and lit candles. These all contain etheric energy. Having plenty of house plants is also said to be a great help. Indoors or out, once you have cast your circle and called upon elemental powers and the deities and stated your purpose, you can chant the following.

Chant for Power

> *Wraith power of wind be mine*
> *And wraith power of flame*
> *And wraith power of clear Water*
> *And wraith power of stone.*
> *Wraith power of Earth and sky*
> *And from realms under Earth,*
> *Be in my blood and bone.*
> *Be in my hands and heart*
> *And each and every part.*
> *Wraith power, now fill me top full.*
> *In wild strength, answer my spirit's call.*

Chant this once and then repeat the last two lines, over and over, while turning or dancing in a circle. If space, circumstances or inclination do not allow dancing, you can use your index finger to draw a small circle horizontally. Make a continuous circling motion with a diameter of, say, a few inches. Carry on with your chanting and circling until you feel at one with the etheric power that is carried on all the elements. If you are a beginner, feel that this may be so. At first it can be hard to tell. Do not worry about that but proceed with trust.

Finish by putting your hands on or just over the main spell materials that you are using, such as the the herbs. Visualize or state that the power is now pouring into them from your hands.

Next, you can cast your actual spell. When you have finished, it is correct to make a formal ending by thanking the powers who have helped you. Say:

I give thanks to the Mother Goddess
Of all Creation
And to the Horned God
Who is nature's guardian,
For their blessing upon my work,
May I now go forth
In love and wisdom.

Add: 'I give thanks, also, to the spirit/s of [the plant, stones, holy well water or whatever it is that has been of assistance in that particular spell].'

At each of the four directions, and at the centre, say, 'I give thanks to the guardian spirits of [name the appropriate power]. Hail and farewell.'

Finally, surround yourself with an imagined sphere of blue light, or state that it is there.

You may be more comfortable with less formal ways of raising power. When you are experienced, you can do it swiftly, especially outdoors, by visualizing the power of the place where you are working coming into your body. This works wonderfully if you are somewhere supercharged, like a seashore or a forest. Many people, wherever they are, like to visualize themselves as a tree, with a very long root that goes into the Earth, as far down as Her molten core, from which they draw power. I must say, this does not work for me, but it is quite popular, so it may be effective for you. However, if you are just beginning in magic, or if you are feeling less than your best, then the more elaborate method of chanting and calling on elemental powers is more reliable.

Another way, for those hedge witches who work with familiars, is to ask your spirit companion (whether faery, animal or person) to bring you some etheric energy. They will then transfer it to you, in much the same way that a spiritual healer transfers healing energy.

Here is a suggested task. Get a hardback notebook to use as your 'Book of Shadows'. This is a modern term for a magical journal or notebook. Hedge witches of the past did not usually have these: it is clearly not an ancient tradition. Most of our forebears could probably not write. But we are in a literate culture now and have minds stuffed so full of facts and figures that remembering all our magical chants and spells and rites can be difficult.

Begin your magical notebook with an account of casting a circle, in the following stages.

1.   Assemble all materials needed and decorate the altar, as necessary (e.g. with seasonal plants or with ornaments in tune with your spell's theme).

2.   Sweep or purify the working area if it is indoors.

3.   Make an opening statement out loud or in your mind, e.g. 'I cast this circle in the names of . . .' etc.

4.   Cast the circle with a wand or your fingertip.

5.   Invoke the elemental spirits of the four directions and the centre.

6.   Invoke the deities.

7.   State the purpose of the spell.

8. Chant (or use another technique) to raise power.
9. Pour energy into the spell's main physical focus.

Go through the preceding chapters and find all the words and actions which accompany thses nine stages. Write them in your magical notebook, and lastly, write down the words for a formal ending, a thanking of powers.

This circle-casting procedure can be used as the foundation for any magical rites. It can be adapted for work outdoors, for example by using a flat stone as an altar in a woodland clearing. It can even be done silently in your mind, without any ritual regalia, if you are far from home or wish to work magic discreetly in a public place, like a park. You can alter the wording to suit your own style. For instance, those drawn to working with faery familiars may like to call the four directions by the names of the four faery 'cities' of Gorias (East), Finias (south), Murias (west) and Falias (north). Traditionally, each of these places has a ritual object linked with it. These are a knife for Gorias, a staff or spear for Finias, a cup for Murias and a stone for Falias. You can still place a cauldron (such a common motif in faery lore) at the centre. Do not use a knife made of iron or steel (or do not place one upon your altar), since it is said faeries do not like this metal. If you can, display one made of another material, such as slate, glass, flint, silver or copper.

The psychic William Sharp, writing as Fiona Macleod in the late nineteenth and early twentieth centuries, claimed that the fifth faery city, at the centre, was symbolized by 'a glen of precious stones'. I do not know quite what I make of this myself, but crystal or glass, which are or are like semi-precious stones, are often mentioned in faery tales (glass slipper, castle or island, that kind of thing). So the idea may be a valid one; it may betoken a more etherialized form of being (as compared to that of ordinary stones) and so fit quite well with the theme of Ether.

Continue to use your Book of Shadows to record any

magical tips, spells, rites or ideas which come your way. In order to do the spells which I am about to suggest, extract the procedures and words for each one from the relevant chapter, leaving out my comments and explanations. As you transcribe them, you will come to understand each spell far better than if you merely read it. Make any alterations or additions which make the work more in tune with your circumstances or your own spiritual orientation. Make it your own.

Spell-casting is not a fixed process. There are rules and guidelines, but it is in no way like assembling a model, following the instructions on the box! It is more like sculpting something as an artist would do it, according to their individual vision. This takes initiative and a respect for your own autonomy, which may be why natural magic (as a long-term spiritual discipline) tends to appeal most to the more free-spirited type of person.

7 Spell to Banish Bad Spirits

Not long ago, a woman to whom I was giving psychic counselling raised an important question about magic. Is it right, she wondered, to cast spells that affect other people? Is this not manipulative? She herself was suffering from a form of emotional and verbal abuse within her marriage, and yet hesitated to use any magic to prevent it. Her sufferings continued, in spite of the fact that she was a hedge witch and could have done something about it.

I believe that this woman was right to take the moral issues surrounding the use of magic so seriously. Anyone using hedge witchcraft must ask the question: 'Who am I, to shape behaviour patterns in other people without their knowledge and consent?' However, I would not hesitate to do such work if all other approaches (such as discussion or confrontation) had already been tried and had failed. I would not hesitate, providing my spell targeted a 'spirit' or trait which was universally acknowledged to be destructive, and not a person.

Today, there are many New Age techniques being taught and written about which are designed to make us immune to oppression from others. These range from the idea that if you think positive thoughts about having fair relationships nothing can go wrong to the view that if you maintain boundaries, remaining very clear and straightforward about what you will not put up with, then others will treat you well. There is a certain amount of truth and usefulness in such theories and practices, but each rests upon the idea that it is the victim of abuse who needs to change, not the perpetrator; we seem to blame the victim. While it is true that a victim may, in some instances, have colluded with the oppressor, this is not the whole story. Indeed, in some circumstances, the idea that the victim is in any way to blame is downright offensive. Witchcraft, by contrast, has always recognized that spells might need to be aimed at changing the abuser, by ridding them of the 'demons' or bad spirits which cause the trouble.

I would have no objection to magic being wrought upon me to prevent my abusing others, if I were guilty of that. However, it must be remembered that what is perceived as a destructive trait or tendency (a bad spirit) by one person is not necessarily so to another. One person's idea of 'sexual peversion' may be another's 'joyful sensuality'. What appears as 'aggression' to one person may be 'healthy self-assertion' to another. Seen in this light, the attempt to use magic to alter someone else's behaviour is an outrageous interference with their Goddess-given autonomy! This is the problem which was rightly referred to by my client. It concerns us all if we use magic.

On the one hand, if we do not attempt to banish the demons (that is, the spirits and thought forms of destructive traits) from our world and from our relationships, then they will go on damaging our lives, undermining our health, souring our happiness. On the other hand, to judge and then magically meddle with another person's psychic ecology is a most serious form of abuse in itself.

I believe that we should do the work of banishing bad spirits, but within strict guidelines. Here is an example of the kind of spell that falls within these.

Spell to Banish Abuse from a Relationship

Cast a circle if you are working formally. In some way, call upon the elemental spirits for psychic protection and assistance. Invoke the deities whom you worship. State the purpose of your spell. Then raise power, using the chant I have suggested, or any method which you prefer. Pour the power into a candle.

Light the candle and say: 'I name this the flame of love between [the other person] and myself. It is fed by [list the things which keep you together, such as shared aims, passion and good companionship].' Also mention some of the other person's good points, the things that you love about them. If the list is short or simply irrelevant because the wounds have gone too deep, the cruelty has been too extreme and you just want to get out, then do not proceeed with this spell. Conclude with something like, 'But the love is over' and pinch out the candle. Obviously, this could be a very painful moment of realization but it is better than forcing yourself to go on. However, if you still feel the relationship is worth salvaging, continue, saying, 'May this flame burn brightly.'

Take a piece of paper cut roughly into the shape of a doll (a kind of 'poppet', as witches say). On this doll, write some of the harmful things which have been said or done to you. Then, holding it in both hands, say:

I name you 'Cruelty'.
You are the spirit of cruelty,
Which causes pain. And you shall be gone.
As I burn you in this fire,
So shall all cruel remarks and actions
In my relationship with [name the person]
Become a thing of the past,
A smear of ash.
I banish you by desire
That love shall continue.
And I invoke, in your place, light and warmth
Of kindliness. Be gone now, in flame and flash!

Burn the poppet in the flame, catching the ash in a dish of pottery or glass – not plastic. (It is best if the poppet is not too big, as you do not want to set off the smoke alarm.) All of it must be consumed but at some point you will have to drop it into the dish, so that you are not scorched. If the piece that you were holding is still unburnt, light a match or taper from your candle flame and burn the rest with that.

If you are a man doing this spell to banish the cruelty of a female partner, then you might want to give the poppet a skirt, or something else, to suggest it is feminine. Similarly, if you are a woman banishing a male partner's cruelty, you may want to give it a more or less male appearance. But a demon of cruelty is neither masculine nor feminine. It can be in any of us. Therefore, it is best to give it a sexually neutral appearance. This makes it much easier to remember that you are dealing with a demon, not a person. On these grounds, you may want to avoid giving it a human shape of any kind. Designing a poppet in the form of a fantasy monster could be your solution. Give it fierce eyes and a snarling mouth.

After burning the demon of cruelty, spend some time visualizing or else describing to yourself the relationship in a state of kindliness, with all abuse gone. Think of the kind of remarks you would like to hear and the ways in which you would prefer to be treated from now on. This may be painful, in view of past suffering, but try to do it as best you can.

Place around the base of the candle some roses or dried rose petals, also some lavender and meadowsweet or pennyroyal. Rose is, of course, the herb of love *par excellence*. It is also said to promote compassion. Lavender, in magical lore, can help to prevent cruelty, especially if worn as a perfume consecrated to that special purpose. It is a herb of peace, as is meadowsweet. Pennyroyal is said to prevent quarrels. Any of these herbs can be used fresh or dried. Your aim in placing them around the candle is to help invoke such qualities as may increase 'the light and warmth of kindliness', the spirit you want to draw in, to replace cruelty.

Let the candle burn down. If possible, do not extinguish it. You may have to do so if you are going out or must go to bed, but in that case relight it as soon as you can.

End the rite by giving thanks, as described in the preceding chapter.

If you feel that you are the one with the tendency to be a bit cruel, then reword the spell as appropriate for banishing a demon that is yours alone. You can still burn the candle as something like 'the flame of love and goodwill', whether or not you are in a relationship. This flame is potentially within us all. And who knows how an invocation of it may manifest in your life? Perhaps you will find that it is newly kindled within you, or that someone else's love for you unexpectedly helps to drive out the demon.

Because the aim of this spell is to banish a demon of cruelty, it can only take effect if one or both of the people within the relationship *is* being cruel. In the case of verbal 'cruelty', the offending remarks may merely be sharp and perceptive, and may be justified. In this instance, the spell will allow them to continue. In no way is anyone being manipulated to change behaviour that the other party dislikes, but that may be appropriate.

Moreover, the spell-caster does not hesitate to banish any such tendency from themselves as well. The spell is worded so that cruelty 'in the relationship' is targeted. In this way, the witch can work with genuine justice, invoking guidelines for the future by which she or he must also abide.

Some people may find such a careful attitude unnecessary. Witches have always, in traditional terminology, banished demons. Nowadays, we may talk about spells to remove destructive traits but it is the same thing in the end. Our practices are derived and descended from those of the tribal or shamanic wisewoman or –man, for whom the driving out of bad spirits has always been a prerequisite for any form of healing, whether of a person, place, relationship or situation. So what is the problem? And what is the point of having such powers, which can help or defend ourselves or others, if we are too feebly cautious to use them? To hell with all this soul-searching, they say, just do it!

That may be true, but I feel that we cannot be too careful not to take upon ourselves a self-righteous, policing attitude that can be demonic in itself. There has been a great deal of that in the world already. At its worst, it uses physical punishment and even torture to drive out 'wickedness' from other people. The less extreme end of the spectrum can involve demonizing the alleged wrong-doer just because we do not like their politics, beliefs or lifestyle, denouncing people as 'sinners' and ranting in pulpits. Many people have raised the spectre of 'demons' and 'evil', in the past to instigate witch hunts and even to justify executions. These are truly emotive terms.

We have to be very careful about judging the presence of bad spirits in others, especially when our conclusions are to be acted upon in a spell. However, I do not advocate leaning the other way and thus leaving the demons unnamed and unchecked.

Tips for Spells to Get Rid of Bad Spirits

Name the demon as a negative trait, e.g. 'greed'. Do not name it as a person's habitual style of conduct, e.g. 'Anne's way with money'. For who is to be entirely certain that Anne is wrong? If, however, a mistake has been made and Anne is innocent of greed, merely anxious or insecure, then she will not have been manipulated into a change for which she is not ready. The spell will cause her no harm; it will just be ineffectual. Perhaps she is neither greedy nor insecure but sensible and prudent. It all depends on your point of view.

Names are powerful, so try to name the demon correctly. To this day, many witches have a secret, magical name, known only to themselves, their familiar spirits and a few other witches. This is because, worldwide, there has been a magical tradition which states that if someone knows your true name, they have power over you. Some of our faery tales convey the same message (Rumpelstiltskin, for instance). To transpose this into everyday life, it is easy to see that once a group of oppressed people have named the demon that is hurting them, they are one essential step nearer to dealing with it. They have already broken some of its power, by using the true name, e.g. 'racism' or 'intolerance'.

In my youth, people who owed money to someone else were always described as being in debt. Nowadays, debt has been renamed 'credit', its true name largely forgotten, and much greater numbers of people are now a long way under its power. To name something bad with accuracy is something we always need to do, in everyday life as well as in magic. This may require careful thought. However, it is not necessary to find the one and only true *word* for something. In many instances, there are more than one. 'Intolerance', for example, can be called 'bigotry'. 'Pride' may be called 'arrogance' or 'conceit'. It is the meaning which counts, not the exact word. And sometimes a phrase will do. To split hairs over exact shades of meaning may inhibit the process of naming. For there may be various words by which to name a bad spirit, in any one of the world's languages, and any one of them may be adequate.

Choose or make an object for your spell that has qualities akin to the bad spirit you wish to banish. Then transform it. For example, you can smear one of your own garments, such as a shirt, scarf or hairband, with mud, to represent the humiliation caused by 'mud-slinging' (slander, name-calling and so on). Then wash it ritually in soap and salt water. (Salt is a psychic purifier and the magical aim would be to purify you of humiliation.) Then dry it and keep it somewhere safe, with some buttercups wrapped inside it. This herb can help to strengthen your own inner sense of your real value. If none are available, use borage, fresh or dried, to invoke the courage to believe in yourself, in spite of unpleasant gossip.

As you deal with your symbolic object, say the spell that you have composed. This is said to be more effective if it rhymes. Unrhyming verse will do, but there is something about a rhyme that is as conclusive as a bolt sliding shut. It seems to bar the way against anything other than your spell's success. A near rhyme can be just as effective and is sometimes easier to find. For example, in the muddied cloth spell, you might say something like:

As my muddied cloth becomes clean
So I remove humiliation's stain.

This drives the spirit of humiliation out of yourself but the spell can also be worded to drive it from somebody else, if you like. It can be adapted.

Name the spirit you are calling upon to replace the demon. For instance, in the spell to remove cruelty, the light and warmth of kindliness, a composite being, is called upon to replace the bad spirit. In the muddied cloth spell, spirits of self-worth or of courage in the face of attack are possible replacements for humiliation. Never leave a void. Always name something good in your spell, to replace the bad thing. Nature abhors a vacuum, as they say, and if you do not invoke a chosen spirit to replace the demon, it is possible that something as undesirable as that which you have banished may take its place.

If the spell is provoked by a conflict between yourself and somebody else, always include yourself within its scope of action. For example, if you are banishing a spirit of bullying, apply the process to any such demon you may be harbouring, as well as that which possesses the other person. This makes for a spell based on justice and helps to guard against the manipulation of another person, because you have not attempted to impose any standard of behaviour on them which you would not also apply to yourself.

I did not say all of these things to my client, I am afraid – not even a fraction of them. But now I know what I wish I had said.

Some demons are easy to identify, others are not. Either way, many pursue their aims in a much larger domain than the purely personal areas of our lives. That being so, it seems clear to me where some of our work may lie as hedge witches in the future – in helping to banish the global demons of greed, injustice, hatred, intolerance and revenge, not to mention the demon of manipulation, which is so often seen at work in spin doctors' versions of current events.

8 Spell to Counter an Ill-wish

Now for another difficult and, perhaps, unpopular subject: the vexed question of hexing, i.e. wishing ill upon somebody, cursing them, thereby causing unhappiness, ill-health, bad luck or loss. Stereotypically, those who practise natural magic are (or were in the past) supposed to be doing this sort of thing all the time, dispatching our victims with cold-blooded abandon to all kinds of suffering: wishing a murrain upon neighbours' cattle, causing people to waste away, muttering dark maledictions in tumbledown cottages, in spite or jealousy.

Of course, these stereotypes are nonsense and always were. But that does not mean ill-wishing doesn't exist; it is all too common. Nor does it mean that witches are never guilty. Like non-witches they can succumb to temptation. Unfortunately for us, however – and this is the real point of this chapter – a witch may be more vulnerable to being ill-wished than most people. This may come as a surprise, for are we not meant to be tough as old boots and protected like bank vaults, psychically speaking? I am afraid that this is just one more stereotype.

There was a traditional country test for a witch, a part of British folklore now, which illustrates the point. It was used by ordinary people and not, so far as I know, by the Church in its witch-hunts. If you wanted to know if your neighbour was a witch, you secretly nailed one of her or his footprints to the ground. A real witch would soon start limping, feeling injured in the foot whose print had had a nail driven through it. But a non-witch would be unharmed. Of course, this is a ridiculously unreliable test, for a number of reasons. But what it indicates is that a witch was thought to be more likely than a non-witch to be sensitive to the effects of magic being practised against them – or if we are honest, to the effects of a curse – for what else is banging a nail through somebody's footprint to make them lame?

Witchcraft appeals, quite obviously, to the more psychically sensitive. For if you are good at sensing atmospheres, sometimes have some foreknowledge of events and notice spirit presences in nature, then things like magical healing or hedge witchcraft might well be a part of your life. Yet that very sensitivity, which is shared potentially by most magical practitioners and also by many artists, writers, mystics, musicians and many other people, as well, is also the very thing which can make you more vulnerable to what used to be called 'bad vibrations', and to any ill-wishing directed at you.

On the other hand, we witches generally are more able to notice psychic trouble than most people, and to reinforce our psychic protection accordingly. But we are not infallible. Oh, that human dream of infallibility – of being so absolutely invulnerable to all danger and every kind of threat that we never suffer again! In reality, which is where we live, we each do the best that we can to deal with trouble and to heal the future (our own or somebody else's) with spells, however and whenever the need arises. But there is one thing about which we can be certain: a magical remedy exists for any kind of problem, including ill-wishing. Although we cannot say we will never be vulnerable again, we can at least say that we will always recover. We can always bounce back, the ill-wish removed, the effects gone – and quickly.

Before describing the kind of magic that counters an ill-wish, I would like to stress that the habit of wishing ill upon those with whom we are angry is a not uncommon human failing. Almost anyone might do it – it is by no means a problem confined to the activities of 'black magicians'.

A friend of mine, another solitary witch, once took part in a television programme about present-day practitioners of magic. Afterwards, she received an enormous postbag, about 500 letters. She told me that most of them were from people who had been ill-wished by someone they knew and desperately needed advice on how to remove the hex. I have myself, received such letters and phone calls.

Those who ill-wish others are not necessarily witches. Nor are they always evil nor even especially nasty-natured. Most often, they just do not realize how effective an ill-wish can be. They do not think it really works. They simply vent their feelings by saying things like, 'I hope she loses all that money!'; or 'I hope he really suffers. I hope he never has any real friends again! I hope he ends up entirely alone and isolated. Let that happen to him. It's what he deserves!'; or 'She ought to be abandoned when *she's* pregnant! Let her find out what it feels like.'

Ninety-nine per cent of the time, these things are said in just the same way that we might swear when seriously upset. It is not that people do not mean what they say; at the moment of speaking, they mean it with every fibre of body and soul. But they do not believe it will actually make any difference. They think they are relieving their feelings and nothing more.

I know of a case in which a person made a very specific ill-wish, concerning a particular type of physical injury, which came true to the last detail. The perpetrator was appalled, guilt-stricken and, quite frankly, astonished! He knew he had psychic abilities but had never expected this ill-wish to be effective. (The victim did not know about what had happened. She merely thought she had had an unfortunate accident, for no special reason.)

Lest we become judgemental about this, it needs to be remembered that almost anyone, pushed far enough, made to suffer acutely enough, could be tempted to wish suffering upon their oppressor in a moment of despair. It is often a question of how far we have been deprived of our hope and strength or how severely we feel that our lives have been damaged. However, that does not mean that all ill-wishes are justified. Pettiness, jealousy, vindictiveness and the pointless holding of grudges are some of the less admirable reasons why an ill-wish might be made.

Today's witches, as a matter of fact, may be less likely to fall prey to the temptation to curse someone than other people, because we know how well it can work. We know also that, by the laws of magic, that which you give out rebounds upon you, three times increased. In other words, if we wish suffering upon others, we can expect to suffer three times as much in the course of time.

Very strangely, in view of this, there have always been some witches prepared to curse other people on behalf of someone else, in return for payment. They are much like mercenary soldiers, who will kill people for pay, without having any interest in whether they are helping to fight for freedom or allying themselves with a monstrous tyrant. I have never met this kind of mercenary witch, so I do not know how they cope with the thought of reaping what they have sown. Perhaps they do not believe that they will. (Such fantasies do a lot of harm in more than one area of life.)

It is interesting that ill-wishes can be so powerful and immediate, when other more worthwhile objectives can require elaborate spells. Why can we not wish for a million pounds as successfully as some people wish that others should have a bad time? The answer lies in the huge emotional charge and the focused will-power that are behind any ill-wish. If we really did want a million pounds so badly, we could (if there were no predestined or karmic reasons why not) wish it into our lives quite easily. But most of us are just not that intense about serious wealth. We might think that we are, but yearning wistfully to win the lottery (and, meanwhile, panicking about how to pay our bills) is just not the same as the white-hot raging determination with which people utter an ill-wish. The only other area of our lives in which we are inclined to match it is when we are in love and want to seduce someone. Rage and desire – powerful forces, in which the whole of a person's psyche can become involved, with definite results.

If you are, or have ever been, in a situation like divorce, family conflict or a battle for child custody, or anything else in which feelings run very high, then you might like to think about whether you have fallen prey to someone's ill-wishes. This is not to suggest that your ex-partner, your relations or colleagues are evil-minded. Merely that rage at a perceived defeat can vent itself in spiteful utterance, particularly when the perpetrator does not believe that this will really hurt anyone.

In past centuries, people believed to be guilty of ill-wishing were accused of 'witchcraft' as though the practice of natural magic and a tendency to be vindictive went hand in hand. Furthermore, innocent wisewomen and cunning men were often scapegoated for someone else's guilt. And people who were envied for various reasons, such as their sexual attractiveness or their success in life, were also falsely accused. In fact, large numbers of people went to their deaths, being hanged or burned at the stake for 'witchcraft' in medieval Europe because of a supposed connection between natural magic and malice. Paranoia ran so high that almost every run of bad luck was put down to someone or some spirit having worked 'witchcraft' and spoken a curse. Clearly, this was ridiculous, since bad things can happen for a huge number of reasons, without any ill-wishing having occured. But, caught between the Inquisition on the one hand and the feudal overlords on the other, and frequently in conditions of the most appalling squalor, our medieval ancestors were understandably unbalanced in their perceptions. We need to remember, however, that curses are not a fiction and that bad wishes can be made about us by people who are unhappy, or by bad spirits, such as those referred to in the past as 'the unseelie court' of faeries in Scotland and as 'dark elves' or 'bad faeries' elsewhere. Most faeries, by the way, are friends to us, and they feature prominently in the following spell. But there are corrupt beings in the Otherworld, just as there are in this world.

If you suspect that some kind of suffering may have been wished upon you, at some point, then a spell can be cast to counter it and so restore your life to its proper balance.

Spell to Counter an Ill-wish

Have ready a bowl of dried rosemary, juniper and black-thorn leaves. (If blackthorn is unavailable, you may use dried nettle instead.) Upon the leaves lay a length of thin black thread, about 9 inches long. Also have ready an incense burner, charcoal block and matches; alternatively, you can use an essential oil burner and oils of rosemary, juniper and pine – or just one of these oils if you have to economize.

Cast a circle and invoke the deities in your own way, or as described in earlier chapters. Say, 'I am here to cast a spell to counter ill-wishing.'

Do the power chant, 'Wraith spirit of wind be mine' etc., while spinning or dancing widdershins.

If you have a wand, carry it with you while chanting and, at the end, raise it high above your head. Then lower it, to point into the herbs you have in the bowl. Pour the power raised by your chant down the wand into the herbs. Do this by the effect of your thought. *Think* that is where the power is going and will it so. (If you have no wand, make the same ritual gesture with your forefinger, pouring the power along it and into the contents of the bowl.) Next, start a charcoal block burning. Begin piling the mixed herbs on to it.

If you cannot be in a room with incense, because of asthma or some other health problem, you should instead direct the power into a mixture of water and essential oils of pine, rosemary or juniper, or all three. But you will still need to have a bowl with at least one of the herbs in it, as well as the black thread. Have the oils already in the burner and the candle lit before you begin the rite. It is not practical to do it later, if you have to remove the dish of water and oils, in order to light it up.

When the incense or oils are rising as smoke or steam, say:

I invoke the powers of the web of fortune, the bright faery spirits of a just future, they who serve truly the Mother Goddess, in Her aspect of Queen of Fate. I invoke the faery weavers of a bright future of natural justice, against all ill-wishing from spite or hate.

Pause and then add:

Justice be done,
Bad fate revoked,
Curse turned around,
For I invoke
You fair weavers –
Answer! appear!
You fair weavers –
Answer! draw near!
And bless this magic,
As it is fair.

When you sense that the spirits of fate – faery weavers – are listening, speak to them in your own words. Out loud or in your mind, speak of your fears that suffering has been wished upon you. Ask their assistance in restoring your health and happiness and adjusting the web of fate, in accordance with justice. Ask that they return your life to its rightful state, unaffected by any ill-wish.

Pause, and listen very carefully to any message or feeling about what they might want from you in return for this help. It could be something that is clearly relevant, for example, is there someone whom you could treat more justly, or someone for whom you could say a regular blessing, to help them thrive against unfair odds? But even if the message fails to make any sense to you, then you should still undertake to do as they ask, providing the request you believe they have made is completely harmless.

If you do not hear or sense anything, then simply offer whatever feels right to you. However, you should not make any promise to the Fair Ones, unless you are sure it will be kept. Tradition says that any vow made to the faeries is a most serious matter. Breaking it brings repercussions, in the form of bad luck.

Breathe in the healing, transformative incense (or steam). These herbs have powers of cleansing and hex-breaking. Rosemary attracts faery presences, juniper is linked with justice and blackthorn with destiny. All three are banishers of negativity, as is pine, if you are using the oils.

Ironically, blackthorn is a herb much associated with formal ill-wishing and bad magic, but it can be used for some other purposes. It offers strong protection *against* curses – a case of fighting fire with fire. It appeals to me to use it in a spell against ill-wishing, as something which has a sinister reputation is turned to a constructive purpose. But if you have to substitute nettle, that will work just as well.

Next, pick up the black thread from the bowl or cauldron. Pass it three times through the smoke or steam. Then hold it fairly taut, with one end pointing towards your heart and the other away, in other words, at a right angle to your body. Say:

Such bad fate that to me was sent
By ill-wish or malicious spell,
I turn, as I turn this thread,
From me and mine. So all is well.
Let it return to the sender!
But only that which has been meant.

Fold the thread in half, with both ends pointing away from you. Thus, magically, you return the suffering to the person who has ill-wished you. (And since you have not named them as anything but 'the sender', it cannot be sent to the wrong person.) You have now created a new pattern in which, just like the thread the energy of ill-luck turns around, straight back to where it came from.

You may want to add something like this:

By illumination, let this turn
To a fruitful end, a lesson learned,
A problem with the answer clear
Or something that has a ready cure
For whomsoever sent this curse.
Let it return to good effect,
By understanding and this verse.

Tie the thread so that the two ends remain together, lying in the same direction. Return it to the cauldron or bowl for a while. Then rest, as you feel yourself returning to normal, to a life free of the effects of ill-wishing.

Now burn the black thread, catching the ash in another bowl or on a plate. Later, put the ash and the remains of the herbs on the garden, or on the earth, somewhere. If you use a lightweight thread, it will burn easily. Black embroidery cotton is ideal. Try not to use wool, as it smells horrible when it burns.

Thank the fair weavers for their help. Conclude your rite in the usual manner, with thanks to the deities and elemental spirits.

You may be wondering about that last, optional bit of the spell when, if you feel enough forgiveness for the ill-wisher, you add an invocation to the effect that the curse shall return to them, but softened, transformed. Traditionally, a curse cannot just be cancelled. Once it exists, it must run its course somehow. That is why we return it to the sender. A curse, like a line of poetry, cannot be unspoken, once it is uttered. However, it can be modified by adding other words after the event. As the story of Sleeping Beauty tells us, a curse can be made less deadly. Briefly, for those who do not know it, this story tells of the life of a princess, who is cursed with an early death, by a faery (a fate spirit) whom her parents have offended. But another faery, while not able to undo the curse, changes the effect, turning it to what may be seen as an initiatary process, involving a long sleep and a sexual awakening. (Faery tales contain much Pagan wisdom and mystery teachings, albeit sometimes in a distorted form.)

So the last bit of your spell aims to do something similar, to transform the pattern of bad fate – this time, from point-less suffering to a life lesson. However, you may feel that forgivenes is out of the question just at the moment. You may be unable to speak the transformative verse with sincerity. If that is so, then you should leave it out.

By the way, the same process can be applied to any ill-wishes that we ourselves may have made, perhaps without realizing that they come true. Using the same herbs or oils to invoke the fair weavers, it is possible to say something like this:

I call back to myself the effects of any ill-wishes that I have made. If I have wished any person dead, may the death of my own malice result. If I have wished ill-luck, may my own worst schemes suffer. If I have wished unhappiness, may my heart break for the pain of the world. May any ill-wish I have made return to me, to destroy not my life or well-being, but my illusions about myself, and so set me free.

This can be said formally, in a full magic circle, or, if you prefer, informally in your mind.

Not all those whom we call faeries concern themselves with the patterns of fate. Nevertheless, there are such faeries and these attend to the laws of justice as well as to fate-weaving and prophecy. They are not 'flower spirits' but beings from an otherworldly aspect of life, which is interwoven with this one. They serve the Mother Goddess in Her aspect of Queen of Fate, the Faery Queen. This belief was held in England right up to the sixteenth century when, according to Barbara Walker in *A Woman's Encyclopedia of Myths and Secrets*, faery godmothers were still asked to attend a newborn child, 'For to set the babe what shall Befall him'. She also tells us that, in the twelfth century, the Bishop of Exeter was recorded as being annoyed that people invoked the Three Sisters of Fate, asking them to give a good life to any infant. These three sisters, the Triple Goddess of Fate, were known throughout Europe. In Scandinavia they were called the 'Norns', in Greece, the 'Moirae' and in Britain (among other things) the 'three Cornwall sisters', one of whom was Morgan Le Fay.

This Triple Goddess, with Her attendants or representatives, is said to control fate. She is the force of karma, the laws of cause and effect by which we reap what we have sown, the solid fact of having to live with the results of our decisions, both individually and as a species. It is certain that no injustice, such as an ill-wish, can continue, once She has been invoked. Even as a homely faery godmother's assistant so in tune with both the gentleness and the ragged mystery of hedge witchcraft, Her decree is indisputable.

Like almost any spell in this book, the one to counter ill-wishes can be done on behalf of somebody else, with appropriate changes in the wording. Simply hold the black thread horizontally, running from right to left hand, rather than away from you. Neither the supposed ill-wisher nor the victim need be with you, at the time. But it is very important that the ill-wisher should never be named. It is enough, when turning the black thread, to direct that the effects of the curse shall now enter the web of fate, to be returned wheresoever they really belong. That way no mistake can be made and no innocent third party can suffer through receiving the full force of a returned curse when they have not uttered one in the first place. And it is all too easy to think we are sure who did it, and even to believe that a psychic message has pointed the finger at somebody, and that cannot be wrong. It can. No one's judgement is infallible, and as for psychic perceptions, they are notoriously unreliable when anger, fear or any other strong emotion becomes involved. It is never wise to make the assumption that we are certain about who has ill-wished somebody. For myself, I would need to have heard the curse spoken with my own ears. Anything else would be hearsay or guess-work, and only an amateur would proceed on that!

It has always been a part of the work of those who prac-tise natural magic to counter the effects of ill-wishing or to advise on how to do so. Traditionally, the methods used in Britain to banish curses were quite strange, at least, from the medieval period onwards. They were said to involve activities like standing on one leg while holding some pig's dung and reciting some prayers. Another popular method of negating bad magic seems to have been to advise the victim to touch a dead body, preferably one which had been executed, or else to touch something associated with execu-tion, like a hangman's noose. (The writer Thomas Hardy used this theme in his short story 'The Withered Arm' in *Wessex Tales*. He maintained that the main protagonists in the story were known to him and that the events in it were real.)

Medical practices from the same centuries now also strike us as brutal or inappropriate. So I suppose it is no surprise that magic could be rather bizarre to our modern minds. The *Zeitgeist* does tend to prevail in all walks of life. Of course, I do not mean to imply that all magical practitioners and all doctors were barmy or brutal, merely that the style in which we do anything tends to be coloured by the mood of the times in which it is happening. Personally, I think we are just emerging from many centuries during which almost everything, from sexual relationships to education to medi-cine and magic, was distorted and damaged. The reason for these distortions was threefold: the terror caused by the Black Death, the brutality of the witch hunts and the depri-vations of the mass of people, caused by the greed of the overlords. Now the mood of the times in magic inclines us to focus upon the mysteries of mind and spirit, all the inner mysteries of dream and vision, the inner meanings and subtle essences, such as those found in flower remedies and homoeopathic potions. We are influenced by ideas from such disciplines as psychology and neuro-linguistic programming. Therefore, our present-day magic is gentle and subtle in its physical manifestations.

9 Spell for Psychic Protection

Prevention is obviously better than cure. So let us have a look at magic for protection from psychic attack. It seems that in every culture on Earth, the need for this has been recognized. From the Indian practice of sewing small mirrors on clothing to reflect back the bad magic of an ill-wish to the Italian hand gesture for averting the 'evil eye' and the British practice of carrying small equal-armed crosses of birch or rowan wood bound with red thread, people throughout the world have taken steps to ward off evil spirits or any ill-will. (In Britain, the carrying of birch or rowan wood talismans is no longer common practice, but it is what our ancestors did, and what some present day Pagans still do.)

One method that seems to be popular now is to construct a psychic barrier or 'shield' around yourself by visualizing one, in order to shut the bad things out. A variation of this is to place seals upon your psychic centres, that is, upon the chakras, which are now familiar to students of many psychic and magical systems derived from Eastern mysticism. Any of these ideas can be useful in an emergency, as when one is suddenly faced with someone whose psychic atmosphere feels unhealthy. They are also very useful for aiding the transition between magical work and the everyday world, so that the harsher vibrations of what passes for reality are not too distressing when we are in a sensitized state. But, as a long-term strategy, they leave much to be desired. The first problem is that they fade fairly quickly, unless they are constantly maintained by fresh visualization. The second is that, if you kept a psychic barrier around yourself permanantly, it would cut you off from too much that you actually need. Psychically speaking, it would be like living your whole life inside a space suit or a suit of armour. It would block out things like the loving thoughts of your friends and the sustaining power of the Earth's subtle energies. Believe me, it is not a good idea, and can even make you rather ill. In another analogy, it is rather like sealing all doors and windows in case of toxic fumes, and then leaving them sealed, permanently.

Gentle variations of this technique, such as visualizing yourself surrounded by a blue sphere of light like the Earth's own atmosphere, do not shut everything out, any more than Earth's atmosphere blocks out the effects of Sun, Moon or stars. But effective, long-term psychic protection requires more than this. And you may need psychic protection often, if your work or position in life are inclined to arouse jealousy or any other obsessive emotion in other people. Those whose jobs have glamour are especially at risk – artists, performers, clairvoyants, life coaches and teachers of practices like meditation, yoga or, of course, magic. Others who are traditionally held to be in need of psychic protection, are people whose circumstances have made them more vulnerable than usual – women in childbirth, newborn babies or those in situations of acute rivalry or conflict. I would add that anyone who is especially sensitive to psychic atmospheres or other people's moods would be well advised to gain psychic protection.

As Serena Roney-Dougal tells us in her book *The Faery Faith*, researchers have discovered that even if someone only thinks about you, with an intense emotion like anger, your bodily processes can be affected. And this happens whether or not you are conscious of what they are thinking, and whether or not you are in their presence. They can be some distance away from you, but the results will be just the same according to experiments conducted in some universities. It would seem that we are all connected on a psychic level, affecting one another, for good or ill, far more immediately than we realize. Those who are in good health and not seriously affected by stress are the least likely to be damaged by this. Therefore, the most obvious form of psychic protection is to look after your health with simple measures like eating and sleeping well and getting enough exercise.

Within the realms of natural magic, there are many plant and mineral talismans that help to ward off negativity. These can be worn, carried or used in spells. Plants include birch, rowan, St John's Wort, thyme, rosemary, betony, dill, fumitory, garlic, comfrey and many more. Some of the minerals are flint, amber, citrine, agate, quartz, fossils, stones with a naturally occuring hole in them, jet, marble and salt.

What kind of spell can be cast to give you greater immunity from the attentions of unkind spirits or other people's angry, resentful or belittling thoughts – or even actual ill-wishes? It helps to have a strongly woven, positive fate so powerful and creative that it overcomes any psychic hostility – a positive future that you yourself have preordained, using magic. This can be set to prevail against any psychic damage done to your health or your future. Your fitness and chosen way of life can be so strongly invoked that they will exist continually in spite of anyone's psychic hostility or undermining thoughts. Such a spell can create a bright, strong picture within the tapestry of fate, a picture of a life of health, success and happiness. You can then enjoy these things in future on your terms, your own choices, effort and life lessons, as distinct from what you might have experienced because of psychic sabotage.

I believe Native Americans say that we 'walk a crooked trail' in life if we are influenced by others' negative feelings or manipulations. If so, they are right. A spell which lays out in advance our own choice of life story or 'trail' is the strongest possible protection against this influence. So whether or not you believe literally in bad faeries, evil spirits or the adverse health effects of other peoples' hostility, you may still feel that such magic can heal your life, if only on a psychological level. As a psychically sensitive fay and hedge witch, I know that it is far more than psychological, though it is that as well. However, so long as it works for you, whether you share my view or not does not matter.

Most attacks which are mounted upon us are both psychic and psychological. (The psychic, in such instances, is merely the more subtle resonance of the psychological, anyway.) Sometimes they are carried out by people who think they have our best interests at heart, sometimes by people who think they have a right to coerce or co-opt us. This frequently includes parents and other relations, including children, or a partner or ex-partner.

It is, of course, vital to examine our own behaviour towards other people in this respect. We, too, may be guilty of attempts at psychic aggression or coercion.

Cultural trends can also be felt as a collectively maintained psychic pressure about how we should or should not live, what we should or should not believe, etc. The first part of the following rite addresses these issues as well as the problem of psychic manipulation, ill-will and so on from individuals.

Spell for Psychic Protection

Set some rowan berries burning as incense, or use essential oils of thyme and rosemary in an essential oil burner. Cast a circle as usual, requesting the presence of elemental spirits and invoking the deities.

Say, 'I am here to cast a spell of protection for myself,

against any ill-will or psychic negativity.' Use the wraith power chant or something similar, and dance or spin deosil. Direct the power into a fossil with your wand or your hand, and also your strongly held intention, as previously described. Remember, 'Energy follows thought' is a maxim for all workers of magic. Our psychic energy flows in the direction of those things about which we think, especially if there is a strong desire that it should do so.

Your fossil may be of any kind and should be placed in a cauldron or bowl, at the circle's centre, from the start of the rite. Pick it up and hold it in your cupped hands. Say something like this:

Spirit in the fossil stone,
You show life from long ago.
In your house of memory,
You hold a ghost of plant and bone.
Life's pattern and a seed that's sown.
I link your power with my own.

Pause, and feel the same life force contained in the stone flowing also within your own life, in your body. The same evolutionary Earth power that shaped the creatures or plants now fossilized is also in your own blood and bones, heart and soul, and unfolding life story. You, like any life form, are a part of the Earth's own body and spirit, expressing your own small measure of Mother Earth's or the Horned God's own creativity. This is an awesome gift – and power. It is the power of evolution itself, in Earth, to survive, adapt, create, learn and know. This power far transcends all petty attacks on your spirit or on your choices. Experience yourself as aligned with this power, as a child of the Earth, who is priest or priestess of a creative destiny.

Now place the fossil upon your heart, in recognition of this connection as fact. Say:

By the blessings of the Earth, our Mother,
And of the Horned God, nature's guardian,
I am at one with the free will bestowed
Upon me before worlds were made.
Thus, I choose freely,
Who has the best right to choose,
About my own destiny.

And, as firmly as the life pattern
Is set in this fossil,
So shall be set the best fate
That can be mine,
According to my own choices.
This shall prevail
Against abuse or spite,
Manipulation or any evil
By day or night.

Touch the fossil to a beach pebble or a piece of limestone or slate, or whatever the local stone happens to be in your area. Say:

I draw my life's pattern here [indicating the stone, not the fossil].
I draw with the power that is Earth's magic and creativity.
Nothing shall change this pattern, unless to improve it. I draw my
destiny [here, name your intentions for the motifs of your future
life, e.g., 'A life of adventure and joy, in which I give and receive
fulfilment in love', 'A life in which I fulfil my best potential for
health, happiness and success', 'A life in which I both learn and
teach wisdom and also apply it in all situations.']

Please note, this spell is not only for young people. However old you are, you still have a future. However, your requirements in later life may be more like the following: 'A life of serenity, with all my mental faculties intact, to the end, in which I experience deep spiritual communion with the deities.'

Each of the above life patterns expresses general intentions. But you can be much more specific, if you like. For example, 'A life of service to the community, as a school teacher'. However, it is much better to say something non-specific, about which you are certain, than to name a destiny about which you may have unresolved doubts.

Remember, too, that there may be experiences already predestined for you – meetings, partings and many other kinds of event, either happy or sad. Your present spell will not overide or subvert these. Indeed, it cannot, for many of them will be woven into the web of fate by our own choices or for karmic reasons, before even we are born. But what this spell can do is to ensure the best-case scenario – a fulfilment of your free creative choices – in and through whatever life has in store for you. This will overcome any psychic attack upon your fate, from any person, group or bad spirit who does not like you or your choices. And the reason your choices will prevail is because you are aligning them with the great power of Earth Herself.

Note, also, that you have stated that the pattern cannot be changed *unless improved upon*. This means that, should you decide upon an even better future, you can do the rite again at a later date.

Using another piece of stone, a sharp one, scratch something that symbolizes the life pattern you want into the stone you have touched with the fossil (not into the fossil itself). For example, if you want a life of inner and outer beauty, you might draw a stylized flower, which might also symbolize, if you wish, the life of a creative artist who makes things of beauty. One symbol can include many things. You might inscribe a pentagram if you intend to live a life dedicated to magic or a caduceus, if you want to enjoy good health or be a healer. However, your symbol does not have to be one that is universally understood, just so long as it is meaningful to you. And it will almost certainly not be artistically drawn, but this does not matter. Even a rough representation will be all right; it is the intention with which you draw it that matters, symbolizing a certain kind of life, a chosen pattern.

You may also draw two interlinked symbols if one does not seem to convey all that you have said, or a main one surrounded and embellished by other signs. But keep it simple and memorable.

Say:

This is the spirit pattern of my life,
Now set in stone.
This is the pattern that I shall live,
In heart and soul and blood and bone
This is the pattern that protects me
Against manipulation or evil strife,
The pattern of my own power, my chosen life.

Now say a word or phrase which sums up your chosen pattern and put the stone you have drawn upon back in the cauldron, with the fossil on top of it. Add, 'So may it be.'

Sit with your hands, palms downward, upon the ground. Visualize, or describe in your mind, your best possible future. Include as much detail as you can. You have now, as they say, protected your boundaries, against any psychic manipulation or attack.

Later, you should bury the stone on which you have drawn your symbol. But keep the fossil safe upon your altar, if you have one that is always in use. Otherwise put it somewhere else that is safe. As regularly as possible – daily, if you are feeling pressurized – hold it and say your chosen word or phrase of destiny. Then use your wand or finger to inscribe a pattern in the air, the same one you drew on the stone that was buried. This will continually strengthen and reinforce your protection.

In magical lore, all fossils are held to be psychically protective, as well as being seen as containing magical power. By the word 'fossil', I do not only mean things like amonites, which bear the imprint of an early life form. Amber and jet also count, for they are pieces of fossilized resin and wood from ancient forests. If you cannot obtain them, or any obvious fossil, you could use a piece of limestone or marble, since they are composed of the crushed bones and shells of ancient sea creatures. Chalk, a type of soft, earthy limestone, is also all right. You could actually use it to draw upon your second stone, although the marks would soon fade, unlike a scratched design. Chalk is also not satisfactory as a talsiman of protection. Coral could be used, but only if it is very old. It is wrong to support the harvesting of live coral, for environmental reasons.

We can each psychically become a victim if we are willing to be one, or if we are temporally exhausted and made vulnerable by a life crisis like divorce or bereavement. An existing pattern of good destiny protects against this. It is like having a web site to your own design, which contains the film script of your life. This site is yours alone, under your control. However, you can still get the equivalent of spam. So now for the second part of the rite, although here the analogy breaks down, for it is not a magical firewall that you are going to create next, but a relationship with a protective spirit.

If necessary, pile on more rowan berries for your incense or check the water level in your essential oil burner. Rowan incense is not only protective but attracts helpful familiar spirits, some of them faeries. These may be requested to become a kind of guardian, and will do so if you treat them with respect. Such alliances between witches and faeries are well attested in folklore and tradition. Above all, faeries have always been said to instruct witches in magic. (I have long been the fortunate pupil of one such faery woman, myself.) But their assistance is given in many ways.

Some of the presences you attract may appear in a vision or in your mind's eye as faeries in something like human form. Equally, they may be creatures, such as the well-known faery hounds who have white bodies and red ears. But the faery realm contains so many diverse types and species that you may see anything at all. Of course, if you are not clairvoyant, you will not see them, but most people of even slight sensitivity can tell when there is a spirit presence close by, whether they see it or not. On calling for a protective faery familiar, you may feel a slight tremor run through your body, as the spirit enters your aura. Or you may simply start to be aware that someone is with you. This is no more difficult than sensing the psychic atmosphere in a house, once you put your mind to it.

Do such beings really exist as something more than a fantasy – Elven men and women and creatures, from a sort of parallel universe, which we call the Otherworld, who are objectively real? I believe that they do. And our Pagan ancestors, worldwide, have certainly always thought so. But even if you do not, you may still wish to continue the rite, regarding the faery guardian as, perhaps, a watchful protective aspect of your own psyche.

Not everyone believes, literally, in faeries but they do tend to believe in us. However, for this rite, we need to drop the idea that they are always tiny and sweet. Traditions, worldwide, tell us that these beings can as easily appear large and threatening. For example, there is the black faery dog recorded in English folklore. If it walks alongside you, it is said to protect you from danger. But if you meet it coming towards you, this may be an omen of death – your own or that of somebody close to you. The black dog, which is said to have been seen by many people, can look almost as large as a Shetland pony and rather sinister.

You are about to make a request for protection to the faery realm. The being who answers may not be a huge black dog, but it will not be a dainty little flower spirit, unless you have made the wrong invocation!

If you are a beginner, try this part of the rite in a spirit of hopeful experimentation. But remember that faeries do have a strong code of conduct. By this, I mean they are said to expect courtesy in exchange for their favours.

Breathe in the incense smoke or oils three times, then face to the west and say something like this:

I call now upon the kind realm of faery. Let one come this way who will watch over me. In the names of the Mother Goddess, in Her aspect of Good Faery Queen and of the Father of Life as the Elven

Lord, I call to one who will be my guardian, wheresoever I am and at all times, keeping me safe from psychic harm and protecting me.

Sit or lie comfortably and close your eyes. If you are able to visualize, picture a woodland, where there is a spring flowing out from a stony hollow surrounded by trees. Annoint your brow with the water from this spring in your imagination, then stand back and watch. From behind a huge jutting rock by the spring you will see someone appear – a bird, an animal or some other kind of creature, a faery man or woman or a faery presence as a gust of wind or shape of light, like a hovering coloured cloud. It could be anything.

Ask this being if they are willing to help you be safe from every kind of psychic pressure, threat or danger. If you feel that the answer is 'yes', then ask for a name by which you may call out to them, in future. The first thing that you hear 'with your mind's ear', in imagination, is the name you should use for them. If you hear nothing, decide on a name. A simple description will do, like 'hawk protector' or 'silver light' or just 'faery guardian', based on whatever you see or believe that you sense. In time, you may build up a clearer idea of this being and then another name may occur or be given to you.

If you cannot visualize or sense anything, then tell yourself a story of the woodland grove and a guardian who meets you there, appearing through a faery portal from behind a big rock. You may take it on trust that, since you are telling the story as a ritual act, it will resonate in psychic realms and will produce a result.

Try to sense what this being requires of you in return for help. After all, nobody wants to act as a permanent guard dog and not be given, as it were, a place by the hearth and some food. Our ancestors in Britain and Ireland did make offerings of food to the faeries in centuries past, in exchange for assistance with many kinds of work. Some present-day Pagans are reviving this practice. Bread, cream, milk, fruit, grains or honey were popular gifts – particularly cream or honey. On the other hand, your protector may want something that is unconnected with food, for example that you always wear a green, red or white thread around your neck or wrist, in honour of the faeries (these are the colours said to be favoured by them in their own attire), or that you make a wild area in your garden, hospitable to native plants and creatures. Faeries like wild places. The old mocking cliche 'there are faeries at the bottom of my garden' could actually become true, if you want to make them welcome there! But they may not be gauzy and ethereal; real faeries are linked with the primal forces. They may be gnarled and potent as an old hawthorn tree, and quite as spiky.

If you do not hear anything psychically about required offerings, decide upon something which you feel is suitable, and then include it in the story which you are ritually speaking. For example, 'I feel the presence of the faery guardian close to me and I offer always to wear something green, in her or his honour.'

Such stories have a way of springing to life and can develop an unexpected twist in the telling, which turns out to be just right. You may find that magical story-telling is a most powerful gift that you had not realized you possessed. It is certainly not a second best or substitute for psychic seeing or 'trance journeys' but a major magical technique in its own right and one that I feel is rather neglected. It is best to start very simply with it, expecting to say the bare minimum, and then see what happens.

When you are ready, stand up and face west again. This direction corresponds with faery realms in magical lore. Say, 'I give thanks to my faery guardian for the offer of continuing protection. May we now walk the Path together, in harmony and friendship.'

If you do give food or drink, tradition says that the faery

will take the spirit essence of your gift daily, and the remaining solid substance (now etherically depleted) can be put out on the garden.

Finish your rite in the usual manner, with thanks to the deities and the elemental spirits. As soon as possible, bury your symbol stone, put your fossil in a safe place and make the first offering to your faery guardian. But do not leave it at that. Draw your life-symbol daily with your wand or finger, reminding yourself what it means and so affirming it. Build a relationship with your faery guardian by talking to them in your mind whether or not you can hear answers initially. For instance, ask them to guide you in all your dealings with other people and also in things like your choice of route, while travelling. They need to know you are still interested in having them around, long after the rite is a dim memory. Otherwise they lose heart and leave you. If you feel you can sense some guidance from them, then always act on it, providing it does not go against ethics or common sense.

You are now psychically protected, unless you meet situations where you can sense something of immense evil and terrible strength. After all, there are many evil events and deeds in this world, and these each have their own corresponding psychic energy field and attendant spirits. Think of serial killings, or of Hitler's concentration camps. What psychic energy would such things have? Of course, it is best to avoid going near places where psychic energy fields are likely to be evil. But if you come acoss something that is truly terrifying, it is best to do what everyone else does, all over the world – call on divine protection, cry out to the deities. I call on the Goddess using a prayer made up on the spot. Then I chant the following, repeating it until the danger is past:

Goddess be within me, with your healing spell,
Goddess be within me, making all things well,

Goddess be within me, healing all with love.
Goddess be within, before, behind, to the left,
to the right and below and above.

If the threat feels very intense, I also call upon the Horned God, He who is not only guardian of nature but leader of the mythic Wild Hunt, that is said to remove the souls of the dead to the Otherworld. I ask Him to remove the bad spirit, entity or energy field to where it can do no harm and may also be transformed into that which is in harmony with life. But it is very important never to name any living person in connection with evil when calling upon the Wild Hunt. The Horned God, in this aspect, really does have to do with the realm of the dead and to ask him to remove an actual person could amount to murder. (Actually, it is said that He will remove the person calling upon Him, if they have made an unjust request to remove someone else. So it could be more like suicide.) The Pagan deities are not at our beck and call. Tradition holds that genuine natural justice is Their province. If we invoke Them, the response may be swift and immediate but it may not accord with our own limited ideas or self-centred desires. For some reason, I find this deeply comforting.

10 Spell for Transforming Destructive Feelings

One of the most upsetting aspects of any kind of life crisis is the emotional and psychological anguish which can result. Our own feelings, which we must bear as best we can, are often most painful. For example, after a job loss, there are not only practical matters to attend to: there are also a serious lowering of self-esteem and an increase in insecurity. Someone who has been physically assaulted in the street and then robbed, may feel a loss of confidence in their own judgement and also in their world. After a betrayal by a trusted partner, most of us are likely to feel anger, grief and humiliation. Usually, it is best to allow ourselves time to express these feelings, and to give ourselves permission to feel whatever we feel, without necessarily acting on it. This way, things like fear, anger or grief can run their course without harm. But when there has been a long-term problem (for example, a pattern of sexual or emotional abuse within a family or marriage) then feelings of pain may not be released before they have become destructive. Anger or grief may turn to extreme bitterness or to self-punishing tendencies. It can seem almost impossible to express the depth of the pain and sense of injustice we are containing.

If you have ever been severely wronged or abused, you will know what I mean. You will also know that the prison of degrading bitterness into which you have been cast just seems like one more aspect of the harm that has been done to you (and it is).

There are also times in life when one problem seems to pile upon another. Taken individually, they may not seem too terrible, but coming in quick succession they overwhelm us. There just does not seem to be time to come to terms with any of them. Added to this, we are still required to go on coping with practical matters like housework, childcare and earning a living.

These situations can be very dangerous. Feelings which we have not had time fully to express or to act upon constructively or, if necessary, change, can stagnate inside us, becoming unhealthy and therefore a further source of trouble. For example, clean anger can degenerate into vindictiveness. Fear can turn into irrational phobia. Placatory gentleness can become weak submission. Honest grief can transmute into whining self-pity. Moreover, when feelings are entirely suppressed (because they are seen as inconvenient, shameful or just too agonizing to face) then depression or even physical illnesses can result. Feelings often need healing, and urgently.

Natural magic has many cures for log-jammed, suppressed or stagnant feelings. Herbs like willow, hawthorn, blackthorn, ivy and wormwood spring to mind. And the element of fire is a frequent resource in magic for this purpose; people may burn things such as an unsent letter, into which they have poured their negative or painful feelings, so that the fire may transform them. However, in the spell that follows, I am going to suggest working with spring water and crow feathers, for a good, strong, specific result.

Water represents, among other things, emotion, in magical lore; it corresponds to feeling. This makes sense. We shed tears of joy or pain, and when we are happy we say that our 'cup runs over'. 'Still waters run deep' is used to describe a quiet person who has profound feelings. Life without feeling is said to be 'dry' and 'arid'. Any person described as a 'dried up old stick' is thought to be without passionate feelings. Moreover, water changes its crystaline structure as a result of exposure to any strong expression of feeling from people in its vicinity. This assertion, together with the experiments which proved it, is explained in a book called *Messages from Water* by Masaru Emoto, and it is relevant to the spell that follows.

If possible, use fresh, local spring water for your magic and collect it in a glass bottle rather than plastic. If you have to buy spring water, it should also preferably be bottled in glass if possible. Glass is said to maintain the living energy of the water more completely than plastic; that is to say, the wraith is much more present in an organic container. Another option is to collect rain water in a glass, pottery or wooden vessel. Only use tap water as a last resort.

The second ingredient for the spell is a crow feather. This can be from any member of the crow family – crow, raven, rook etc. The type of magical power associated with each is similar to that of the others, at least for present purposes.

If you for any reason, cannot find any feathers, use a hawthorn twig, as this tree is linked with crow magic in traditional lore. Failing that, you can fashion a makeshift, symbolic crow feather from wire and black thread, or whatever suitable materials you can find. It does not need to be a work of art but it must be something you can dip into water, so black paper will not do.

Crows, ravens and the like are all connected, in northern European lore, with what are called 'Dark Goddesses', that aspect of the Great Mother which is concerned with death and rebirth. Hers is the realm under the earth which pertains to burial of the dead. Hers is also the transformative, purifying process by which dead bodies break down to become part of the earth, to feed plants and other creatures along the food chain. Hers, too, are the carrion birds that pick dead bodies clean, changing a possible source of disease into their own healthy living flesh. Old, corrupt emotions can also be changed by Her processes which, on a psychological level, can work through dreams, magic, sexual release and self-expression.

A witch does not fear this aspect of the Lady, understanding that She is the magic of deep healing and also of rebirth. Carrion birds, graveyards and darkness do not strike us as terrifying or demonic, but as sacred symbols of a natural alchemy.

One clean, fresh crow feather is all you will need for your spell. But if you find several, you can decorate your altar with them or keep some for future spells. Crow magic has many purposes.

Spell for Transforming Destructive Feelings

Cast a circle. Call upon the elemental spirits and invoke the deities in your usual manner. Say: 'I am here to cast a spell to transform my destructive feelings into life-enhancing and positive ones.'

Use your power chant and channel the power into a flat, shallow dish of spring water. Say, 'May my feelings and thoughts be as clear and life-giving as this water.'

Now pick up your crow feather. Holding it over your heart, say the following words:

I call upon the power of the Lady of Darkness. For She, the Great Goddess, is not only light and the sweetness of dove and lark, but also sombreness, carrion. As a crow, Her spirit seizes whatever is corrupting, to purify it. Her presence has always hovered above battlefields or places of famine and sought out whatever lay dead, on roadside or midden. She makes all fresh and leaves just the white bones, pristine. Nor does She bring disaster. Her will is not to cause untimely death, but to transform both spirit and flesh, after a tragedy, and to bring rebirth. In the same way, She can strip our souls of what is outworn, rank, if we call on Ḥer to bring change. By Ḥer, we may rise on wings of wisdom, despair changed to hope, cowardice to courage, fear to a wise caution, jealousy to celebration of another's happiness, ungoverned rage to construc- tive action, depression to creativity. I invoke Ḥer presence in my life, Dark Lady of Transformation in crow feather cloak. I call upon Ḥer now, to take and change for the better all that which is ill within me. To take my [e.g. bitterness, phobic terror, vindictive- ness, confusion, self-destructiveness] which I now place within this water.

Put down the crow feather and, with your index finger, write upon the water's surface. Write one word or phrase which sums up each destructive feeling you harbour, but do not name more than three feelings, as it is too much on which to concentrate in just one spell. As you write each word or phrase, project its unpleasant meaning straight into the water by the power of your thought. Think it is so and, because water is so responsive, it will be. Your water container will probably not be very large so you may have to write one word on top of another. Think of the previous words as having sunk down below the water's surface. The water's actual physical structure will have retained the feel- ings that each represents, making this, as it were, rather unholy water, for the time being.

Pause when you have finished writing. Now think, instead, about the new feelings and attitudes which you would like to develop. For example, if you have written 'confusion', remind yourself you would like to feel 'clarity' or 'decisiveness'.

Now pick up the crow feather again and say:

As the crow feather writes words of good feeling within the water, so all is well. So shall the mood of the water be transformed, bespelled. So shall it be remade in harmony. And, as this water, so my own soul.

Write as many new words or phrases as you recorded negative feelings. Use the crow feather as a quill 'pen' this time. So if you wrote 'fear' with your finger, for example, you may now want to write 'courage' with the feather. Or if you wrote 'meanness', you may now write 'generosity'.

However, there are two types of transformation and you will need to have chosen between them beforehand. The first and most obvious is the one reflected in the examples I have given above, in which a feeling or trait becomes its own opposite. Thus, hate becomes love, cruelty becomes kindness, etc. If this kind of change feels realistic emotionally, being both attainable and appropriate, then it is the right choice to make. But in some circumstances, it may be best to choose a modification rather than a complete turnaround. After all, if someone close to you has just been violently assaulted, then there is no possibility that raw hatred for the perpetrator (if that is what you feel) can suddenly turn into love. Why should it? Such attempts at 'spirituality' do not really help anybody, and they have no place in the Pagan realism of natural magic. You may wish, instead, to use the energy within the hatred in a constructive way. Thus, you might write, not 'love' but 'pursuit of justice'. Then your feeling of hatred can change into determination to see the criminal legally restrained and, perhaps, your loved one somehow compensated. Vindictive hatred then becomes fair action, something that is of benefit to the community and to the victim.

Meditating upon the kind of change you desire is an essential part of your preparation for this crow magic. To begin the process, it can be helpful to 'brainstorm' about the types of change you might consider. Jot them all down on paper and think about each one carefully before you make your choice.

After writing, pause with the tip of the quill still in the water, and add:

> *Now the script within the water is changed.*
> *Now the feelings within it are rearranged,*
> *Turning from ill to well,*
> *From what causes disease to what brings release.*
> *And as within the water, so within me.*
> *As within this bowl, so in my deep soul.*
> *All is transformed to harmony, clear and free.*

Lay down the feather and pause again, meditating upon the changes.

Annoint your brow with water from the bowl. Using your index finger, draw there an equal-armed cross within a circle. This represents balance, harmony and integration, as well as symbolizing the magic circle in which you cast your spell.

Now sit down with a piece of clean blank paper and a red crayon or a pen with red ink. Write, again your three new, positive words or phrases, the same ones that you wrote with the crow feather. Write also, 'I [your name], live in these feelings, and they in me.' Add the symbol of the equal-armed cross in a circle.

Write this, even if you do not yet feel anything of the sort, even if you still feel bitter, hostile or pessimistic. A spell must have time to work, for natural magic is like nature itself, sometimes slow-moving but deep and thorough.

After the spell-casting, place this magical document under your pillow. Keep it there for at least three months.

It is important that it should be written in red. This draws upon a magical tradition that goes as far back as ancient cave paintings, which often used red ochre. It was also used to stain the bones of the dead. Red represents blood and therefore life. To write a spell or any magical utterance in red has always been thought to give extra potency because of this symbolic correspondence betweeen blood and redness.

You should now spend some time visualizing or describing life as you intend to experience it as a result of your changed feelings. Dwell on your state of mind (calm, assured, purposeful), your state of health (good) and your actions (creative). Go into as much detail as you can manage. If you find yourself slipping back into the negative feeling, repeat the word or phrase describing your new feeling. The same technique can be used in everyday life. Traditionally, words or rhymes of magical impact are repeated in multiples of three or nine, so try saying it nine times or perhaps twenty-seven (three times nine).

Thank the crow spirit for help. Then thank the deities and elemental spirits, as usual at the close of a rite. Afterwards, pour out the spring water on to clean, uncontaminated ground, such as your own garden or at the foot of a tree. Since the water is now magically connected with your own soul it is vital to put it somewhere that feels good. The crow feather can be kept on your altar or stored with your magical equipment for future rites.

11 Spell for the Healing of Trauma

After a severe shock or a particularly horrible incident we are sometimes said to be traumatized. As I understand it, this involves a serious loss of personal power, and happens because a part of our psychic-emotional energy remains so bound up with the distressing event that it is no longer available for other matters.

In shamanic terms (and remember, shamanism, in the widest and least academic sense of the word, is at the root of witchcraft), this is perceived as 'soul loss'. We say, in this frame of reference, that part of the soul has gone away; it has vacated the body and remains 'in the past', at the time when the incident happened, or remains wherever it went at that time. This is not the same as when a person dies. It is more that a part of the soul decides, after serious anguish, that the human world is just too much to bear. It retreats to another place – flies into a rock, becomes part of a tree, hides itself in a deep lake, enters the faery Otherworld or takes refuge in a world of abstractions, forever trying to transcend its agony. For all practical purposes, in terms of our daily lives, it is absent. An important part of shamanic healing is the retrieval of these bits of 'lost soul'. It is necessary work, since we are more prone to physical illness, more tired and less effective in our lives when soul energy is diminished.

Whether you look at this from a psychological or a shamanic perspective, it is obviously a problem that needs addressing after a bad shock or severe suffering. Otherwise, our minds can become in some sense frozen, unable to progress fully beyond the distress. The shamanic approach is described more fully in a number of excellent books, such as Caitlin Matthew's *Singing the Soul Back Home*. But the themes and methods of soul retrieval are easily adapted for use in the spells of hedge witches and may long ago have been an important part of our repertoire, when the roles of shaman, tribal healer, wisewoman or witch were barely distinguishable from one another.

In the past, our ancestors knew that the wild aspect of nature heals trauma. Apparently, people took themselves off to live in remote places if they had been traumatized by a personal tragedy or an abuse. More recently, apparently, Vietnam veterans did the same thing. Some of those who felt that the terrible things they had witnessed had unbalanced their minds simply went off into American forests to live off the land, alone, for a couple of years. This was the prescription applied by their European ancestors and perhaps some of the soldiers had retained a memory of it on some deep genetic level. (Or perhaps all humans know instinctively that this can be an effective cure.) They could not bear human contact any longer and needed the impersonal forces of nature – no more malice, no more evil, just a raw struggle for physical survival in straightforward physical ways.

Since it is almost always other humans by whom we are traumatized, it is easy to see why this would be therapeutic. Besides, nature has other aspects than impersonality. There are also beauty, mystery and the healing spirits of plant, creature, stone, water, wind, sun, moon and stars. These things seem to allow us to settle back into confidence about life, to become strong and peaceful enough for our missing soul parts to return. After all, nature's sanctuaries are where they tend to have taken themselves so if we go and join them there it is bound to be beneficial.

But retreat on this scale is hardly practical for most people, even if it were entirely desirable. Nevertheless, every natural magician knows that spending as much time as possible outdoors, in contact with nature, is a prime healer of body and soul. Walks in the country, lying on the earth, gardening, visits to wild and lonely places – all these can contribute to our soul's welfare. Each is a gradual encouragement to lost and frozen parts of the soul to return into life.

Another form of modern retreat is to withdraw into one's own house and garden, scarcely ever leaving, for years on end. This, apparently, can produce states of extreme psychic and emotional intensity, in which a healing can take place. The relatively undisturbed peace and simplicity of such a life are a part of what makes it work. If such a retreat can be undertaken in a house in the country, so much the better. The person concerned does not need to be living alone for it to succeed, but human contact is kept to a minimum and much time is spent in meditation, prayer, spell-casting and therapeutic art, such as journal writing.

Natural magic also has some specific solutions to offer. There are plants that can become our familiars (our magical helpers) while we are undertaking to heal ourselves or somebody else. One of the most obvious is willow. Traditionally, this plant has a spirit that helps when love is lost, as many a folk song reminds us. Willow assists when we have been abandoned, jilted or betrayed. It is also said to soothe the bereaved by creating an atmosphere in which spirits from 'the other side of the veil', the afterlife, can come close and comfort us, perhaps in dreams or by psychic contact. In the past, jilted lovers or people who had had someone close to them die recently, would carry a piece of willow or wind some around their hat.

Other plants which help are valerian, poppy and lemon

balm. Valerian can assist psychically by relaxing nervous tension. It is a well-known remedy for a troubled nervous system and for insomnia. However, you need to see a qualified medical herbalist if you are planning to use the tincture or tablets for a long time. It was used to treat soldiers suffering from shell shock after the First World War and is very effective. Magically it has a spirit that comforts. And strangely enough, although it smells rather horrible it can also be used in spells to attract love. As a treatment for trauma, it can help to bring feelings of relaxation and reassurance.

Poppy is another plant spirit that is associated with war casualties. As everyone knows, poppies grew on the battlefields of Flanders as soon as the First World War was over, seeming to help restore the war-damaged land. They are also forever associated, in Britain anyway, with the remembrance of dead soldiers, sailors and airmen on Remembrance Sunday. Unfortunately, this means that it has also been tainted for some of us by a certain jingoistic patriotism which has sometimes seemed to gloss over the horror of all those lost lives. However, it is connected magically and mythically with healing sleep. The common red field poppy is associated with the sleep which heals disillusionment and apathy, brought on by a terrible disruption of life, a tragedy or pointless loss. But it is not wise to ingest it as a tea or tincture, except on the advice of a qualified practitioner, as not enough is yet known about its chemical composition.

Lemon balm, which we shall be using, can relieve tension, depression and anxiety. It has also been credited with the power to prolong life.

Recently, when I was traumatized by acute hostility from someone, I decided to tackle my own healing in a psychic manner. I entered a visionary state to go in search of the missing soul part, which my familiar spirit told me was actually the piece called, in an emotional and symbolic sense, my 'heart'. I found it on a beach where I had recently had an upsetting row with someone – or rather on a faery version of that beach, its equivalent in the faery realm. It had entered into a big white stone and decided to stay there. When I asked it to come forth, it took the shape of a bird and flew up and out. Eventually, I was able to coax it into flying back into my body. Not everyone is comfortable working in this manner, which is often called 'astral' or 'path' working. But there are spells we can cast to achieve the same kind of result. And whether you see this literally, as a calling back of some aspect of your soul that has fled, or as a psychological process expressed in the imagery of a waking dream, such a spell provides the psychic and psychological conditions for a recovery, and creates the etheric pattern for emotional healing.

Spell to Heal Psychological Trauma

For this spell, you will need a stone that is clean and smooth. It can be of any kind, so long as you like it, but cleanliness is very important because of the way you are going to use it. It can also be any size, so long as it is not too large to fit easily in your bowl or cauldron, amongst some herbs. It should also have come from a place that is natural, so if you picked it up while out walking, then it should not be from a car park or pavement but from some-where like a field, garden, wood, river bank or beach.

You will also need, in your bowl or cauldron, a handful each of dried willow, valerian and lemon balm (*melissa offi-cionalis*) or skullcap. Burn one or more of these herbs as an incense, or vaporize some essential oil of melissa, valerian or lavender.

Cast a circle and invoke the elemental spirits and deities. Then say, 'I am here to cast a spell to heal myself of psycho-logical trauma.'

Use the wraith or some other power chant. Dance deosil

while holding the stone, and then pour your power into it through your cupped hands. Then stand before your altar (or face north if you are working outside) and raise the stone to chest height in front of you. Say something like this:

Come now into this stone, my soul.
Come from wherever you've flown,
Come into this stone.
Come from Otherworld waterfall, rock or cave.
Come from tree, hill, lake or land under wave.
Come now into this stone, my soul.
I call to you by the caring of Mother Earth
And of the Horned One.
For we will find places of healing, joy, magic, rebirth.
In the names of the Mother of Life
And of the Horned One,
Come into this stone, you alone and none other.
All aspects of my soul that have taken flight, gone or been led away,
I call now into this stone, with welcome.

Pause a while for anything of your soul which may be coming out of the north. Then take the stone around your circle to collect any other parts coming from east, south or west, pausing at each direction. Then approach the centre and hold the stone high, towards the moon and stars. Finally, hold it low, to draw up anything from beneath, in the Underworld.

Do not fear that the soul parts will stay away. After all, they belong to you and you have called to them, so they must come.

When you are ready, put the stone gently among the herbs in your cauldron, with these words:

As the stone is surrounded by powers of healing,
So shall my soul be restored in contented deep feeling.
I shall live whole, integrated, at one with life.

Poppy Palin

Sit or lie down for a while, and visualize or describe the stone as holding a pale golden light. It nestles among the herbs, which are enfolding it in their healing atmosphere. The light begins to glow, ever more strongly, until it fills the cauldron. See the herbs as representing the healing powers of Earth, Herself. See the stone as generating security, acting as a sanctuary for your lost soul parts. Say:

As the stone is a strong home
And surrounded with healing,

119

So shall be my life,
So shall be my self.

Then retrieve the stone and say:

I now call from the stone
All that is my own.
I call each part of my soul back into my body.
Deep in my blood and bone these shall all reside, at one,
In the names of the Goddess and God.

Hold the stone to your lips. Draw the soul light inside you upon your breath. Put a part of the stone in your mouth. Suck your soul fragments down deep inside you, to enter your bloodstream and there become one with your whole being.

Pause to feel the effect. Put the stone in the cauldron.

Next, pour into your chalice, or into a cup, a herb tea made of willow bark, valerian and lemon balm or skullcap. These can be purchased from a herbal supplier but if they are not all available, or if any are contra-indicated for you, then use what you can, even if it is just one herb. I believe they are all safe for most people, except skullcap, which should not be taken with prescribed tranquilizers. Willow contains salicin, a basis for aspirin.

You may pour this tea from a flask which you have kept ready, unless you prefer a cold drink. To make it palatable, you can add fresh lemon juice and honey. A pinch of ground ginger also helps. (Anyone who thinks herbal teas taste horrible will probably change their minds after trying this recipe.) Do not make it too strong; half a teaspoon of each herb will do, or a teaspoon and a half if you can only get one herb. Strain it before putting it into a flask or jug.

Before drinking, place your hand over it and say something like this:

Spell for the Healing of Trauma

I bless this potion by all that is good.
I bless it in the names of the Lady and Lord.
And, as I drink it, so may I receive the cure that I need
For my troubled soul.

Drink slowly, aware that healing will come into your life, as surely as the herbs enter your body. Know that this will enable your soul to feel that life on Earth is worth living. The potion is one of comfort, on a psychic as well as a physical level. It also connects you, via the willow's power, with realms of spirit that hold the secrets of regeneration, repair and renewed inspiration. This last is readily accessed by poets, who have a traditional link with willow. It enables spirits who teach the mysteries of love, death and rebirth to be contacted. And it helps mediums to speak with those who have passed to the other side of the veil. If you cannot obtain willow tea, it helps to stir your drink with a willow twig.

Close your eyes after drinking the potion and turn your attention towards the psychic dimension of life. Can you feel any spirits drawing near to bring healing? Can you sense any kind of spirit message? If so, record it later, in your magical notebook.

When you are ready, stand and give thanks to the herb spirits, the elemental guardians and the deities, so closing the rite in the usual manner.

This spell will not only restore the lost parts of your soul, but also bring soothing and therapeutic contacts and influences into your life. If you are already having psychotherapy (for example, for sex abuse) you may want to see this psychic process as an adjunct to or an aspect of your psychological journey. There is nothing in natural magic which cuts us off from other approaches to healing, be they conventional or alternative. In fact, it can provide a personal foundation for other therapies to which you might want to resort. Or it can serve in its own right, depending on what suits you and what you choose to do.

12 Spell for Justice

What colour is justice? To those who practise natural magic and who love the land and its ancient traditions, the answer is obviously green. It is Robin Hood's colour; we all know that the legendary outlaw, whose aim was to rob the rich and give to the poor, wore green.

Something else famously linked with Robin Hood is the oak tree. And I have an intuition that people may have gathered under oak trees to settle disputes in Britain in the pre-Christian past. Be that as it may, another renowned mythical dispenser of natural justice, King Arthur, also had a strong symbolic connection with oak, since his famous round table was said to be made of it. As anyone who knows their Arthurian mythology will remember, it is to King Arthur and his knights that 'damsels in distress' would appeal for help in obtaining fair treatment – and not only damsels, but all kinds of people.

I raise this subject because, when our lives need healing, the problem of physical or manifest oppression by others may need to be addressed as well as psychic and emotional factors. For if someone is continuing to act unfairly towards us, then it is impossible to be, and to remain, healed until that has been changed. For example, it is very little use to heal our emotional wounds after self-esteem has been destroyed if the same abuse is still going on.

There are many types of injustice, including manipulative behaviour, plagiarism, anti-social behaviour by neighbours and cheating, as well as possibly more obvious things like racism, sexism or religious intolerance. Anything of this sort may call for a spell for justice.

The well-known symbol of the scales of justice represents (among other things) even-handed and balanced treatment for everyone. Green is the mid-point of the colour spectrum, so it too can symbolize balance. It is also one of the main colours favoured and worn by the faeries who, as we saw in an earlier chapter, can be intensely concerned with issues of justice. Their Queen can be appealed to by simply walking out to a place of the kind that is linked with faeries, such as a hawthorn tree, a spring or a lonely hill, and calling out to her for help in your mind, describing the situation which has led to your plea. If your links with the faeries are strong, this may be all that you need to do.

Justice is seen as female. The traditional figure who is depicted holding the scales of justice is a woman, and she connects with Goddesses like Athena, Maat, Nemesis, Themis and Aradia. There are also a number of male figures who represent the Father of Life, the God, in His aspect of natural justice. Within the British tradition there are, as I have said, Robin Hood and King Arthur, also Bran, Math ap Mathonwy and Gwyn ap Nudd. Each is famous for settling disputes or dealing with offenders.

For the record, the spirit of Robin Hood can be invoked especially for matters of justice concerning land, property or money. Bran, an ancient British God, has to do with justice between rival groups or nations, diplomacy, defence and the fair treatment of women. (These are not Bran's only attributes as a God, but they are those which are most directly linked to justice.) Math ap Mathonwy, in the Welsh book *Mabingion*, is a restrainer and punisher of rapists, as well as being aware of the need for a rape victim to be compensated. Gwyn ap Nudd can be asked to remove bad spirits or thought-forms which are exacerbating a conflict.

King Arthur was one to whom his subjects could always turn for help when they were being oppressed. We can still invoke his spirit now, because Arthur, to a present-day Pagan, is much more than an historical or pseudo-historical warlord. He is a figure from British mythology. The earliest versions of tales about him are set in an era that predates Christianity (and are certainly derived from pre-Christian sources). These depict an Arthur with one foot in faeryland, who leads his followers of quest for the original Grail, a cauldron entirely unconnected with the Christian tradition, which is kept in faery realms. This Arthur is timeless and archetypal and represents the spirit which is eternally trying to re-establish the land as a place of harmony, in every era. Of course, his story has been reinterpreted over and again, with Christian additions. But it was told first in Pagan versions which may stretch as far back as Neolithic times. More recently, there have been retellings by Thomas Malory, by the poet Tennyson and by modern authors like Marian Zimmer Bradley. As the image of a benign, heroic protector and a wise judge, he is certainly immortal. We can call out to him, like this:

> *Great Arthur, you who brought to the land fair treatment for all,*
> *you who were known to champion the oppressed and defend the*
> *weak, and who gave fair judgement within your courts, be with us*
> *now, in spirit. We call upon you, who represent the Father of Life,*
> *in His aspect of natural justice, to put right our wrongs. Though*
> *you rest in the Otherworld, let your spirit be among us. And inter-*
> *vene specially for [here name the victim or victims of a particular*
> *injustice, perhaps some person or group known to you] that justice*
> *be done.*

Goddess knows, as a nation we British need to make this kind of plea! But Arthur (and other mythical beings) can also be called upon for help in more personal matters of justice, both here and in other lands. In America, those of

European descent might find his help very useful. People of other races or places might prefer to appeal to a more local figure – someone from the land that they live in or with which they have ancestral connections. This can be done very easily by lighting a candle to the spirit of the figure you have chosen and making the above invocation, or a similar one. However, there are spells we can cast, as well.

Spell for Justice

Cast your circle and invoke the deities. If you are indoors, burn some oak or juniper incense. (Oak bark from an environmentally responsible source can be bought from a reputable herbal supplier such as Neal's Yard, who will supply by mail order from their Manchester branch.) Otherwise, vaporize some essential oil of juniper. If you are pregnant or have a kidney condition and so must avoid this oil, you can use pine. Say, 'I am here to cast a spell for natural justice.'

Use your chant for power and direct the energy you have raised into a bowl of oak leaves (fresh or dried), dried oak bark from a herbalist or oak twigs. Lift this bowl above the altar in a gesture of offering. Say:

> *I call upon the spirits – the fae – of natural justice to hear me now. You who come in the names of the Great Mother as Queen of Destiny and of the Father of Life as Lord of Justice, I call upon you to intervene, that justice be done, in the matter of conflict between myself and [name the other party]. I offer to you this oak. And I offer my heart for faery judgement. I offer my own heart to be weighed and judged, on the same terms as I call upon you to judge of another/others. Assist me now, in the spell I am about to cast, that justice be done.*

Have a small stone ready on the altar. It should have a rough surface, and should not be soft or crumbly, but something like flint or granite which symbolically suggests a certain harshness. Pick up the stone and say:

Creature of earth, I name you as the hardness of heart within [name the person, group or organization] which seems as stone.

I name you as the hardness of heart within [repeat the name or names] which does me/us harm.

I name you as the hardness of heart within [repeat the name or names again] by which hurt is done.

Take the stone round your circle and hold it up at each direction, and at the centre.

Face the altar again and say, 'These are the wounds caused by the hardness of [repeat the name or names] which I now describe before spirits of justice.' Describe fully, but as concisely as possible, the different forms of hurt, harm or injustice you have received from this person or persons, or which you believe you have received.

Now hold the stone in your non-dominant hand (the opposite to the one you usually write with). Pick up a length of green string or thread from the altar, with your other hand, and hold it high in offering, saying, 'May this represent the power of restraint.'

Sit down, holding the thread and stone. Lay one hand on the stone, in your lap, and say, 'By my allegiance to faery powers and by my use of the green thread, I bind you from causing me any further harm whatsoever, for ever.'

Bind the green thread around the stone, tying frequent knots in it, until the stone is enclosed in a kind of net. This is much easier to do if the stone has a rough, or jagged surface, for then it will not slip. Say, 'As this stone, so [name the peron]'s hardness of heart, bound by restraining powers of natural justice, to do no more harm.'

Pause, then add:

I bring you to the spirits of natural justice to be changed and taught. May you be given fresh understanding and all that you need to grow in harmony. May hardness of heart be transformed to gentleness, rewrought! So may it be.

Place the bound stone in the bowl of oak. Lay your hand over it again and say:

May you become, not hardness of heart, cruelty, but rock-solid kindness and honesty. And if I am also at fault, let all that I have

invoked for you, happen also to me. Or, if I have misjudged you, let
you go free. But let us each/all receive justice.

Now for the next part of the spell. It is normal, after any
injustice which has caused injury, to look for some form of
compensation so that it may be put right. Say, 'I ask for fair
recompense for all my woes.' Visualize or describe to yourself, the kinds of recompense you believe you deserve. This
does not invlove dwelling upon the other party's imagined
future discomfort. Vindictiveness has no part in real natural
justice. And vengeance is not the point of this spell,
anyway. Instead, concentrate on ways in which your own
heart or way of life might be healed. Think of any special
favour which you believe you may need from life, from fate,
in order that the balance may be fully restored for you. Here
are some examples:

1.   a pay rise or promotion at work, if you feel you have been
treated unfairly by a boss or colleague
2.   a stroke of real luck, in terms of money or property, if you have
previously had something stolen
3.   a therapeutic experience or course of treatment, which is both
free and entirely effective, if you have been the victim of either
physical or psychological violence

Try not to picture compensation coming directly from
the person or people who you believe have been unjust,
but from life itself. This ensures that you will not, by
magic, benefit at someone else's expense, in the event
that you have misjudged them, as you may have done –
they may be innocent, or guilty but mentally ill and unable
to help themselves. For example, if it is money that you
need in fair recompense, leave it to the spirits of justice to
decide where, and from whom, this money comes. Simply
picture or describe yourself receiving what you believe
would be an adequate amount. Think of as many of these

compensations as you can and mull over your favourite ones in detail.

It is important to have written down your ideas or at least thought about them, before beginning the rite so that you have felt your way fully into the subject. Apart from anything else, this is a marvellous way to understand yourself and your own agenda, and consciously to define your future goals. The compensation you will receive will depend partly upon these ideas, of course. But remember that you have invoked the spirits of natural justice. They will know what you really deserve and may therefore bless some of your suggestions with success but not necessarily all of them.

Take a new short piece of the same green thread which you used to bind up the stone. Pass it three times through the incense smoke or the vaporized oil. Hold it up at the altar and say:

Here is some of the same green thread which has bound [name]'s heart. This shall be bound around my own wrist, linking my own fate to natural justice, binding me, also, to make a new start. And, for the woes I have suffered, may I receive fair recompense.

Tie three knots in the thread, one in the middle and one on each side, about an inch from the central one. As you tie them, say:

By the knot of one,
I weave in fair compensation.
By the knot of two,
My wish for this comes true.
By the knot of three,
True and entire recompense for harm
Comes straight to me.
And as this harms no one else,
So may it be.

Now tie the thread around your wrist to form a bracelet. Wear it for at least one cycle of the moon (one lunar month), then keep it somewhere safe until recompense has come. But remember, the recompense could appear in an unexpected form. For instance, instead of money, there could be an important, profitable opportunity. And sometimes it may take the more subtle form of inner riches, such as increased creativity or more developed understanding. In any case, keep the bracelet until you feel satisfied.

Last but not least, if there is anyone at all to whom you feel you have been unfair, make a promise to the faery spirits of natural justice to do your best to put things right.

To close the rite, thank the faeries for their help, and thank the deities and elemental spirits in the usual way.

Keep the stone in its bowl of oak until you are ready to bury it. Then put it, together with the oak bark or leaves or twigs, in the earth.

I should say something about the ethics of this kind of magic. The above is a variation on the classic 'binding spell', by which many magical practitioners aim to restrain wrong-doers. It is sometimes done with a 'poppet' (a doll) representing the person who is being brought to justice. Such a spell can be a mistake. For example, you might 'trap' a poppet inside a box to represent a criminal being put in prison. While this may sound, on the face of it, like a good idea, it can backfire. If the other person's magical defences (which may be informal – they do not have to be a trained witch or magician) are greater than your own magical strength, then you may yourself end up in some kind of entrapment. For such a spell can rebound upon the caster, particularly if they are inexperienced. Besides, the person accused may actually be innocent. So if you were to succeed, you would have done them a very great wrong.

In our present spell, the stone stands in for a kind of poppet. But it does not represent the named person in their entirety, merely a trait – hardness of heart. If the spell were to rebound, you would have restrained yourself from acting upon any hardness of heart in yourself. You would also have some transformative lessons, in order that you become more kindly and fair-minded. I do not find the thought of these things happening to me a problem, as I do not want to be hard-hearted and would welcome the chance to change if necessary. So I would do such a spell without hesitation. (In any case, the wording of the above rite actually invites the spirits to deal with the spell-caster on the same terms as they do with the other person.)

Obviously, we have to make sure, in a spell for natural justice, that we ourselves are acting in a way that is entirely just. Offering ourselves for a judgement as stringent as that which we are invoking for somebody else is a safeguard in this respect.

As I said, it is always possible that the person accused has not been unjust, and that the whole thing is a misunderstanding or else the result of manipulation by a third party. In this case, the spell will be ineffectual but harmless. (You cannot bind someone's hardness of heart if they do not have any.)

Other plants which can be used for spells of justice are ash, buckthorn, celandine and juniper.

13 Spell to Consecrate Your Life to a Creative Purpose

A personal crisis, trauma or tragedy can not only be a distraction from your usual activities for the duration of the problem, it can also shatter your confidence and sense of purpose for a long time afterwards. It can even alter your physical circumstances and possibilities for ever. This can make you unsure who you are or what you are doing with your life. At such a time, a spell for the consecration of your life to a creative purpose can bring deep healing. And such purposes are often born from the very difficulties you have suffered. You may, for example, have been the victim of emotional or physical assault on account of your race, beliefs or allegiances or simply for your money. Such a spell can then act as a cry of defiance if you consecrate your life to the creation of a just society.

If you have been attacked for being a witch or some other kind of Pagan, you might want to consecrate your life to bringing a public understanding and acceptance of Paganism. On the other hand, you might simply want to consecrate (or reconsecrate) your life to the practice of using magic to bring many kinds of healing.

If you have had a physical accident or disease, which has left you somehow disabled, your options may not be quite what they were. But this may mean that fate requires you to change and to consecrate your life to some new form of study or creativity.

Alternatively, you may feel as though your life is a little boat that has suddenly been blown off course for some reason. It was going somewhere, but now it just drifts. It is possible to spend a great deal of time in this state – years or even decades. One magical solution is to reconsecrate your life to the purpose you had before you started drifting, or if that is no longer feasible, to a new purpose.

The word 'consecrate' means 'to set apart as sacred', and since a serious abuse or personal loss can make you feel somehow desecrated, a rite of consecration can bring much healing. It can help you reclaim a sense of self as well as of purpose.

When a national disaster such as a war, occurs, many people's personal aims and intentions are put aside voluntarily, 'for the duration'. However, it can just as easily be the gradual attrition of personal problems that wears away our sense of purpose. To return to the boat metaphor, it is not so much that our boat of life is wrecked by either, a personal or national disaster, as that we are delayed in various ports by one thing or another.

The point of a spell to consecrate a life to a chosen purpose is not only so that it may be reorientated on a spiritual, psychological or practical basis, it is also so that we are much less likely to be blown off course in future. Within Paganism, there is a strong theme of offering life force or energy for a good purpose. After all, it happens throughout all nature. For example, when a woman breast-feeds a child, she is giving her own life essence and energy in a nurturing, physical form. And when the crops in the fields, sometimes symbolized in folklore as a presence called 'John Barleycorn', give up their lives, they are reaped so that bread and other cereal foods can be made and the people can be fed. Likewise, the trees give their fruits and berries so that new trees can come into being and also provide nourishment for the wild birds. Clouds give themselves up to the making of rain and then plants can grow. Each life, incuding our own, must nourish others, must serve life itself, if its purpose is to be fulfilled.

But, as thinking, self-determining creatures, we have some measure of choice about what and to whom we give our life energy. Unlike the plants, birds or animals, we may choose not to give any of it to the creation of the next generation. And we certainly do not need to have it all eaten up, as it were, by any person or organization that wants to exploit our time or goodwill. In fact, one of the intentions behind a spell of consecration is to give some protection from anything like that. We can freely choose our own purpose and magically bind ourselves to fulfil it, giving a new twist to the theme of binding, which we have used already in the spell for justice.

One of the plants that symbolizes such a binding is ivy. In magical tradition, it is linked, among other things, with a positive sacrifice. To sacrifice is to make sacred, to give something up to a meaningful, spiritual purpose, if not to a deity. (And within Paganism, many practical activities, such as farming or gardening, are seen as potentially having a strong spiritual aspect. To one who practises natural magic, 'spiritual' does not mean nebulous and unmanifest or sepa-rate from the rest of life.) Ivy can also represent the transformative power which brings an end to an old way of being and ushers in a new one. It is therefore very good for rites which aim to bring an end to an unsatisfactory life pattern and replace it with a better one.

What if you don't know what your purpose should be? What if you are so confused and disorientated that you do not have any idea? In that case, you might try thinking back to the life pattern part of your spell for psychic protection, which might hold some clues. But if you really cannot make a decision, then you may want to postpone this spell until you feel ready for it. However, your confu-sion may not resolve itself over time. As I have said, many people just drift for many years, and are therefore vulnerable to being pushed by the strongest force that is close to them, quite often against their best interests. So I suggest that, if you feel confused, you pick something non-specific, about which you are certain. This is a lot better than doing nothing, and also better than tying yourself to a particular course about which you have doubts. In other words, consecrate your life to a principle rather than to a task or occupation. You could pick something like 'peace-making' or 'healing', which are broad-based, with a wide remit. The advantage here is that such a general dedication gives you a certain direction and protection, but allows time for more specific interpretations of your purpose to emerge later on.

Pick something with which you feel that you cannot go wrong. For example, you might say, 'I've always felt that beauty is really important. It feeds our souls. I want my life to serve that.' Then you can take time deciding upon the specific forms of service after you have done the spell and also change your ideas about them over the course of your life, switching for example from voluntary work as a conservationist to a career as an artist, a craftsperson or a gardener. So long as you keep in mind your commitment to beauty, you cannot make a mistake.

Spell to Consecrate Your Life to a Chosen Purpose

Cast a circle and invoke the elemental spirits and deities. Have with you in the circle two short sticks or twigs and two pieces of plain, undyed string. Also have a long, flexible strand of ivy, a small item which you have worn or carried, like a hair clip or glove, which you find pleasing as a talisman, and another small object to symbolize your chosen purpose, such as a flower for beauty or a little piece of mistletoe wood for peace. You do not have to burn incense or vaporize any oil for this rite but if you want to do so, then

I suggest using peppermint, a herb that can help end destructive patterns and will also dispel discouragement. (You might like to add some other oil to it – perhaps rose or lavender – if you find peppermint too reminiscent of sweets or toothpaste.) Say, 'I am here to cast a spell of consecration of my life to [name your chosen purpose]'.

Instead of raising power with your usual chant or dance, try saying the following instead:

My time and energy have been laid waste
By myself and, often, by others.
My best purposes have been replaced
By the giving of my attention to destructive dramas
In myself and, often, in others.
But all this shall be changed.
I now give myself to [name your purpose].
By this sacred purpose, I shall abide.
So let the song and dance of my life
Be entirely harmonious.
Let elemental spirits assist me in this.
I now change the tune of my own existence.

If this does not express what you feel or is inappropriate for any reason, then change it. Change whatever you need to within the first five lines, so that your own particular problem or past history is described.

Pause. Take your time now to feel your way into your own emotions, when you are distracted, anxious or depressed. Remember the way that you feel when, for example, your time and energy have been taken from you by others' abuse of your goodwill or when you have undermined your own aims by some form of self-destructiveness. Think back to how your body feels when your life is discordant, full of seemingly irreconcilable demands, when you are pulled in two or more directions, until you cannot even recall where it was that you had meant to go in life.

Make sounds which express this state. You may start to take irregular, gasping breaths or quietly wail. You may groan or screech, even howl. The noises need not be loud (unless you want them to be) but let them express discomfort, pain, disharmony. You may simply sing out of tune, droning. However you do it, make some sounds that convey the symbolic tune of your life when it has gone wrong.

When you are ready, begin to let the sound transform into something clearer and more harmonious. For example, if you have been screeching, soften it and drop the note to a lower pitch, without pausing for breath. Then begin to hum that new note more tunefully. Try to let a brief melody develop; it does not matter if it consists of only three or four notes.

At first, your groans or screeches may become a sort of tuneful wailing. Stay with this until you feel ready to make a more melodic, more joyful sound, one that expresses the atmosphere, the resonance, that you want your new, purposeful life to hold. Feel the spirits who assist you, singing along with you now, your singing supported by notes made by the wind in the trees and by oceans, rivers, crackling fires, birds, animals, even the mythical sound of the planets and stars revolving in galaxies. You might hear faery bells, too. Are words beginning to form in your mind? Perhaps a single word might arise, or many, something to be sung that expresses your purpose.

If for some reason you do not want to make much noise, you can dance your life's music, instead. Begin with jagged, discordant movements or anything that expresses your deep frustration or thwarted creativity. Gradually, change to dancing more fluidly, gracefully and coherently. Do this in any way that expresses assurance and joyfulness.

If even dancing is difficult, you could just use the pattern of your breathing. Begin with erratic, shallow breaths to express frustration or anxiety, Then move through to calm, deep breathing, to express your coming into a more harmonious way of life. You can even breathe along with the world's wild creatures in your imagination, or with the trees, or with the sound of faery chanting, hearing it within your soul.

If you are physically active and have no reason to be restrained, you may choose both to sing and dance. As always with hedge witchcraft, you can adapt the basic themes, ideas and suggestions to your own needs and circumstances and to your own style.

By this means, you change the resonance of yourself and your life, as well as raising the power for the magic that follows. At the conclusion of the song, kneel down and place your hands upon the two sticks, which should be at the centre of your circle, lying parallel and touching. They should be pointing away from you, not lying horizontally across your path. They can be any length, from less than 6 to about 18 inches long, and quite stout or no more than twigs. You are going to use them to make a symbolic doorway, so anything will do that suggests this to you. It must, however, suggest a doorway to a place of natural harmony, so the wood must be untreated, unpainted.

Pause. Then gently move the sticks apart, creating a gap about 2 feet 6 inches across, the width of a small threshold. Stand up, and say:

I have opened the door to a life dedicated to [name your purpose]. Bear witness, you guardian spirits of Air, Fire, Water, Earth and Ether, as I step across this threshold, never to return. Protect my commitment. Uphold my purpose. Bring my life to fulfilment, as it serves life. As I pass through this door, I give my life to the service of [name your purpose] for evermore.

Walk through, then turn around and pull the two sticks together to close the door behind you. Tie them with the two pieces of string, one at each end, so that they do not fall apart.

Face the altar. On it should be the long strand of ivy, the item connected with yourself and the item which symbolizes your chosen purpose. If you cannot find anything suitable, you can instead write your name and the name of your purpose on separate pieces of clean paper but it is better to use symbolic objects, if you can do so.

Hold the strand of ivy in your hands and say:

Ivy, you spirit of constancy, fidelity, you who keep the green thread of life through the dark and cold winter, I invoke your power. As I bind [name your talisman] to [name the symbol of your chosen aim], so let me be bound to serve my chosen purpose. Let this bring fulfilment of my best destiny. Let this ensure that my time and strength are used creatively. Let this serve life.

Twine the ivy around the joined objects. For practical reasons, you may first have to fold one item around another or else tie them together with string or ribbon, so that they do not fall apart. But the ivy is the magical binding.

Sit down and visualize or describe your life lived in a new, purposeful, joyful way, a life within the realm which you entered when you stepped, magically, across the threshold, the realm of your own autonomy. Think of the differences that this could make to your attitudes and priorities. How will you change the use of your time and energy to serve your chosen purpose? What are your aims? What will you no longer do, think or believe? What will you do instead? As so often, with this kind of transformative rite, it may help to have made notes on your ideas before you begin. Then you will be able to visualize or describe your new life much more easily because you will already have thought about and resolved any points of confusion. At the end of the visualization or description say, 'So may it be.'

When you are ready, stand up and face the altar. Conclude by giving thanks to the spirit of ivy and to the deities and elemental spirits. The two sticks you used to represent a threshold should later be buried. The two items bound by the ivy may be kept on your altar, hung on the wall above your bed or stored in a safe, special place, whatever feels right to you. If they are on display, they serve as a reminder of your commitment.

For your symbolic threshold, you can use any twigs or sticks that you find. But you may prefer to choose a particular wood that suits your purpose. Look in the lists of correspondences at the end of this book for the magical uses of various plants. For example, you might choose birch, if you are pioneering or reforming something, giving it a new start. Rowan is right if you are dedicated to anything with a practical yet aesthetic element, such as carpentry, garden design or textile art. Heather, a plant associated with gypsies, is good if your purpose involves a great deal of travelling. Reeds are connected with music. Beech is associated with books, historical records and ancient wisdom, and holly with guardianship or protection, such as the protection of a threatened species or of a place, river, stretch of coastland or wildlife sanctuary.

If you have mobility problems and cannot step over a symbolic threshold, then you can visualize or describe it, saying, 'My soul is now opening a door. I walk through it to the realm of . . .' As always, adapt, change or adjust any suggestions in accordance with your own needs, feelings or circumstances. Hedge witchcraft is not a fixed system but a matter of personal and individual creativity.

14 Words of Advice

By now, you may be thinking, 'I have very different ideas about some of these spells', or 'I can't imagine why this spell is designed like that; if it was me, I would have done something different'. If so, then this book has done its job. For, though there are ground rules about natural magic, just as there are, for example, about writing music, their application is all your own. Nothing in this book is a definitive version of anything. In fact, there is no such thing as a definitive version of any spell – anyone who tries to tell you there is should be treated with extreme caution! As I said earlier, natural magic is an art, not a technology. There can no more be a definitive spell for any particular subject than a final, definitive poem about it. Instead, any attempt is valid, providing the practitioner adheres to the basic guidelines. In the case of natural magic, these guidlines are:

1 *Think like a poet. Construct spells in terms of symbol and metaphor. Use materials and make ritual actions which symbolize your desired result, or which represent the spirit powers upon whom you call for assistance.*

2 *Act like a priestess or priest of nature, regarding nature as sacred and full of mysterious powers and presences – which it is. Design your spells accordingly.*

3 *Treat all elementals, faeries and nature spirits with courtesy. Those who practise hedge witchcraft do not 'command' spirit powers but request their help. These beings will be our friends if we*

treat them well. However, they are known to cause problems for us if we are impolite.

4 Work under the aegis of the most sublime, harmonious spirit powers of which you can conceive, the deities (whether or not you anthropomorphize them). To do so is to invoke a strong protection for your own spirit, as well as a powerful blessing upon your work.

Bearing these rules in mind, remember that hedge witchcraft is still a living thing. It is not a fixed and rigid system but a process of change and exploration.

You may also feel that, for you, other spells in addition to the ones in this book would help you. As a means of healing your own or someone else's life, you may choose a few of mine, picking the ones that are appropriate for your needs and then adding others of your own design. For example, if you want to change your luck (and have already made certain that you are not suffering from the effects of an ill-wish and that your psychic protection is strong), a spell for good fortune would be required. Acorns, violets, clover or honeysuckle are all said to bring good luck, so any of these may be useful in such a spell. Or you might want to do some magic to improve your self-confidence and self-image. You might therefore look into a mirror annointed with juniper oil to banish bad feelings about yourself and speak a positive, affirming rhyme about yourself to your reflection (repeating it nine times). The possibilities are endless.

The main thing to remember when constructing a spell is that you should choose to do something which symbolizes the effect that you want. For example, remove a blindfold if you aim to see through deception and misinformation and burn or vaporize rosemary during this rite, as this is a herb which, physically, can help to clear a confused mind. You should always use herbs, stones, colours or other objects which are associated, in magical and symbolic ways with your theme. There are many books on this subject of magical correspondences and some are listed at the end of the book. You will quite often find that the magical associations exist for good, sound material reasons, as in the case of the herb rosemary which is magically associated with things like clarity and psychic cleansing and which is a mental stimulant and also an antiseptic.

Having worked out what to do and having chosen your materials you might, if you are experienced, cast your spell at once. You may need no further preparation, being happy to improvise your words of enchantment as you go along. Indeed, this is all that is necessary if the spell is quite a simple and straightforward one. If it is more complex, you may want to write out what you are going to say, before you begin. Then you have a chance to plan it most carefully and think about all its implications, both for yourself and for others. And this is a good idea for any of us, however experienced we may be.

When deciding what to say in a spell, remember the following points:

1 Sympathetic magic is extremely effective. This is the technique of saying, 'As I do this, so that shall happen', naming your ritual actions and your desired outcome. I think I have included it in every spell in this book. It is not the only way to do strong magic, but it is a truly versatile and powerful method. And even when it is not overt, it tends to be there as a part of almost any spell, since that is how a new etheric pattern is made, a new picture within the woven web of future events.

2 Spells involving other people should only be cast if you would be entirely happy to have the same spell cast upon you. Clearly, any magic which aims either to change or to suppress someone else's choice of career, partner, religion, friends, place of residence etc. would be an extreme form of abuse. As for using magic vindictively, I think that is fine for those who do not mind having a soul that looks like the classic stereotype of the evil witch – bent, malicious, cackling, covered in warts. Obviously, this is not the way anyone really wanting to heal their life would be advised to go, even when tried beyond endurance. Some things just are not worth it.

3   My own spell-casting style can sometimes be rather wordy; I adore words. Your style may be rather different. What you say could be brief and succinct, while the making of pictures or talismans or the ritual use of movement could play a much larger part.

I should add some words of caution. Although you do not have to say much, it is important to be precise. For example, if you are casting a spell for good fortune, state that your luck should not only become good but stay that way. Otherwise you may end up with just one stroke of good luck in an otherwise unchanged life. (Even that would be nice, of course, But you may be able to do rather better.)

It helps to be just as careful in your choice of spell materials. I would like to tell you about something that happened to me a few years ago. I did not record it in my magical diary at the time, but nine or ten months later. I will just quote the relevant entry. The tale has a mundane beginning but makes a strong magical point at the end.

19 November 2002

Today, the builders are here to mend our roof. They have had to replace some boards, put in a lead flashing and realign gutters. And now they say that the tiles have been spread too thinly by the last builder and that this may lead to problems in future. I do not think they are trying to create more work for themselves in saying this. (A builder would hardly need to do that, nowadays, when they are so in demand.) On the other hand, our surveyor mentioned the tiles before we bought the place and he did not seem to think that there would be a real problem.

If I hadn't used the oak box in my spell for a new home, would this be happening? Would we live here, with these particular worries? I have always felt that you can't be too careful about how you word a spell or about the objects used for enchantment. Well, at least the wording was up to me. But as to the objects, I had to use what was available, as is so often the case, not what may have been ideal. Perhaps if I write about it all, I will begin to understand better.

Last December, when we were living in Bath, our flat had to be double-glazed. (We had no choice in the matter of whether, when or by whom this was done, since the place was leasehold.) Afterwards, I had a strong allergic reaction to some of the materials they had used. So far as anyone could tell, this may have had something to do with the type of sealant. Anyway, to cut a long story short, we had to move out at once and stay with my Mum and stepfather in the Cotswolds. It was impossible for me to remain in our home. My throat felt sore and raw and I coughed continually and felt faint and dizzy.

We had been planning to move house anyway, but not like that! It was an eerie feeling, to be so suddenly and so completely dispossessed. That flat had been our home. And then, within twenty four hours . . .

Without my mother's kindness, we would have had an even more difficult time. In effect, we were homeless. Not under a park bench exactly, but suffering a serious loss. And so it happened that, early last spring, I was sitting disconsolately in a small town at the southernmost tip of the Cotswold area, mulling over my intuition that the district in which I sat, known as Budbury, was full of other homeless beings, besides myself – full of homeless spirits, in fact. I felt Budbury had been a place of strong Pagan magic in the distant past. To this day, it has a well which is perceived by many as holy. A small chapel exists on the hilltop. (It was common practice for the Christian Church to build upon sites sacred to the country's native religion – to the various types and strands of the old Earth-honouring Paganism.) Behind the chapel, along the escarpment, there is said to have been a Celtic encampment. I thought of the spirits attending upon this place's traditions, the spirits of the inherent magic of the Earth, to do with such things as rock and cave and springwater and creature and tree, the same spirits who gathered around our ancestors beliefs and magical practices, in the days of the village wisewomen and cunning men and, further back, in the days of their forebears, the Celtic and pre-Celtic tribal healers. What are these spirits, though? What do I mean by this? Well, my faery familiar tells me they are of two kinds. The first are displaced nature spirits. After all, Budbury has now been built upon. Though many of the houses there are beautiful old buildings, made of the local limestone, they have taken the place of the trees and wildlife that once covered the whole hillside. Secondly, there are those entities which began their lives as elemental spirits of water, earth, air or fire and then became guardians of the magical practices linked with the land. These, like the displaced nature spirits, are now homeless. Such spirits and other displaced ones have been living throughout Europe, she says, for many centuries. Discounted and ignored, except by a handful of local witches, they have makeshift homes in places like old trees and the clefts of rocks. But they are not truly housed because so many of their trees have been cut down, their wells capped or polluted. And some of the holy hills have been built upon, with tarmac roads, as well as houses. On top of that we do not recognize them or honour their existence. Like today's travellers or the remnants of gypsies, they can feel hounded and insecure.

I suppose I was identifying with them. A homeless witch, sitting amongst the tenuous presences of homeless magical spirits. I got out a pen and notebook and wrote this poem.

The Homeless Spirits

Many spirits of the land's magic
Have been made homeless.
These drift within the grey mist,
Unaccounted, aimless.
Or crouch beneath dripping hedgerows
Or mutter in hollow trees
Or sleep in limestone caves
Among mosses and lichen.

This was not always so.

Our ancestors housed them.
Call them back! Call them!
Feed cream and honey.
Give them snug cupboards
Or glass bottles on shelves
As did Biddy Early.
Venerate hollow trees, for their sake.
Dress the wells. Bless the stone circles.

They have work to do.

I don't know quite what I think of some of the ideas contained in this poem – but it just sort of poured out. Biddy Early, by the way, was a nineteenth-century Irish witch, reputed to keep glass bottles in which dwelt some of her familiar spirits. Anyway, having written the poem, it occured to me that I could cast a spell for a new home for us, based upon this very theme. For I could house some of the unhoused spirits of the land's magic and then prevail upon them to find, in return, the best possible home for our own needs. This would bring us a lucky break of some kind in what was, at that point, a very competitive housing market, indeed.

Of course, housing the spirits would mean more than simply finding or making a suitable receptacle and inviting them in. I should also need to make offerings to them, to feed them, as you would a familiar spirit, on herbs or honey or fresh spring water, or to give them a local crystal or something. And I should need to treat them with respect – to remember and honour their purposes (in connection with natural magic) as well as my own – their allegiances to the land. I could then perhaps ask their assistance in any matters connected with housing.

I decided to house them in some sort of box, not in a bottle. So the first task was to house them in a box that was suitable. I have no skills in carpentry, so I couldn't make one. I searched all the gift shops in Bath and in the surrounding small towns for something ready-made, and rejected the many boxes imported from India. These have a connection with India's natural magic because the trees they are made from have grown in that land. But I needed something that had once grown in our local landscape, or at least in Britain to house some magical spirits of the land where I live. On top of that, I couldn't be certain whether the imported boxes had been made with rainforest wood and no one selling them seemed to know, so the environmental implications were dubious. Not much of an offering to the spirits of any land to use wood from what could be quite unethical sources for casting spells! Out of respect for India's spirits, India's ecology, I wouldn't buy one.

There weren't many kinds of box available, really. But I felt under duress to get this spell done quickly, as house prices were rising faster in the country districts (where we wanted to live) than they were in the city (where we had a flat to sell.) So I had to make up my mind.

There seemed to be two choices: a small box, handmade from recycled timber that had once been part of an oak beam, so the label said, in a Devonshire farmhouse; or a large, hand-decorated box that seemed to be made of pine, covered with pictures of gardening tools and flowers. The oak box was sturdy. It had very thick sides, in proportion to its size. It was also beautiful. Against that, it was tiny and had a lid with a cleft across it. Not that the lid was damaged, nor about to break. It just had a sort of gulley across the wood. It wasn't as strong as the walls and made me pause and wonder about the effect of linking it, magically, with our new home. The hand-painted box was large, implying a spacious residence. Symbolically, the decoration upon it suggested to me a house that might be surrounded by a good garden. On the other hand, it was made of thin wood. Both the box and its lid made me think of a dwelling constructed of flimsy, inadequate materials.

I chose the oak box. I didn't wait. It appealed to me for many reasons, not the least being that oak is a good choice for any housing spell. Traditionally, the beams of a strong house were made from solid oak. And the Celtic word for oak, duir, means or is linked with the idea of a doorway – between different dimensions of existence. So the spirit of oak is connected with entrances as well as with the roofbeam. Oak is a wood absolutely part of the landscape, just as a rightly built house ought to be. And oaks, in the past, were meeting places. Gatherings of all kinds were held around them. They connect, therefore, with themes of conviviality or hospitality. And yet the strong oak spirit will bar the door to unwelcome visitors.

Perhaps I might have been able to find a larger box or one with a more solid lid if I had searched further. But I didn't do that. Whether rightly or wrongly, I bought the oak box with enthusiasm, and planned my spell.

My faery familiar began talking about a tiny but beautiful place, with a leaking roof, where she would be quite happy to see us living, and which would result from my spell. I was shocked.

'A leaking roof?' I said. 'You think we should buy a house with a roof that leaks! You can't be serious.'

'It will only be a small leak,' she said. 'And it will quite soon be fixed.'

Right.

I took the box with me to Budbury, at the Spring Equinox. And holding it up before me, I said (according to rough notes I'd made in preparation) something like this.

> I bless, consecrate and set aside this box, by the powers of Air, Fire, Water, Earth and Ether, in the names of the Great Goddess of Fate and of the Horned God of Nature. May it be a dwelling place for spirits who guard the tradition of natural magic. Spirits who work with those who cast spells for healing and harmony, by nature's mysteries, wisdom and creativity. And, as these same spirits are housed by me, so may they arrange the best possible house for me and my family.

I then called them in.

You spirits of natural magic
Who wander, homeless,

I call you into this box
To be housed, again.
You shall enter and leave
At your own free will, evermore.
And I shall honour you
And guard your door.
And as I house you here,
Ꝼouse me and my family,
In a strong house, secure,
Magical and healthy –
With peaceful, friendly neighbours.
As it harms none, so may it be.

    I placed within this box a piece of our local limestone, one found by my son while out walking and bearing a natural formation of quartz crystal on one end. And I added several pieces of beeswax in further offering, and propped the lid open with some twigs from nearby trees.

    Now, here we are living in a tiny but very magical West Country cottage. The walls are surprisingly thick, even for an old building. And we have had peaceful, friendly neighbours so far. Also, we have had problems with the roof, which did leak at first but was quickly mended.

    I think I did do the right thing. We are really enjoying living here. Besides, a spell is not separate from the rest of the web of fate that shapes all our lives. It is cast in the context of our own circumstances and – if it is not to be manipulative or abusive – the needs of others. Circumstances include things like the place and time available to us, in which to work magic, and the actual materials we can get. Over the matter of the oak box, this seems to be echoed by the fact that, realistically, there is only a certain number of houses available in any person's price range, at any given time. But how fascinating that the box and the house we got were so alike in their characteristics, as well as both available at once. This points to a deep magic in life which far transcends anything I might try to contrive to steal a march on things. My ideal is to come into a permanent alignment with that life magic and then flow along with it, creatively. And somehow, over the oak box, I had a small glimpse of how that can happen. (And it isn't to do with New Age clichés about trust and acceptance. It seems to me to be more about noticing possibilities. Creative watchfulness, perhaps that is it? I'd like to be like that all the time. It's a less elevated and more realistic aim than trying to achieve unquestioning trust in a world where so much can go wrong – and so often does. But it works, apparently.)

I think that journal entry clearly expresses what I feel. Hedge witchcraft is not beyond or outside life's reality.

Rather, it is a creative response to what is already happening, an enhancement of fate. In every way, when using it, we are wise to try to flow with the tides of nature and laws of destiny, rather than try to 'control' or fly in the face of them. This is why natural magic is a lifelong quest for wisdom, a spiritual discipline, rather than merely another technique for trying to get everything we want.

But where, in practical terms, does this leave a person who needs to do a spell to heal their life, given that perfect magical words and perfect spell materials may not be always available? I think it leaves them just where I was left with my spell box for housing, recognizing that any well-designed spell brings a good solid result – for which gratitude is the appropriate response – but that the quest for perfection, that is, for the perfect house or perfect life, is an ongoing process. So, while being aware of the pitfalls, we do the best we can. It is a process by which we learn.

This brings me to a further point, which I have made before, but which I think bears repeating. Just one spell can help a lot, but if the problems are dire, a sequence may need to be done. The nature of that sequence will depend upon what was wrong in the first place. Because it is all a question of fresh creativity, every time, rather than doing things by rote. So what I have tried to present in this book is a method which can be altered or adapted in many ways. This is, I think, akin to showing someone how to use oil paints and then saying, 'Now paint your own pictures. They need not be like mine or anyone else's. The choice of subject, the style, the size and everything about them is up to you. And you will need to practise.'

It has been my experience that it is the practice of natural magic, as much as the end result, that heals our lives. The planning of any spell can turn into a deep meditation upon the problem which, in itself, can yield fresh insights. The gathering of spell materials like feathers, spring water etc., unites us with spirit presences within the land. It is, in the most profound sense, a magical experience to collect, say crow feathers from a field or garden for your rites of healing. The actual spell-casting usually brings moments of transcendant communion with spirit powers and these experiences can be ecstatic. And then there is the process of learning more and more about how magic works, how it underpins everything. This is a rewarding study because it demolishes, at once, the theory that life is so random as to be meaningless.

My advice to anyone, beginner or experienced witch alike, is to remember that we who practise natural magic are living guardians of the connection between wild mysteries and human culture. And perhaps the holding of that ground is the most healing magic of all.

Appendix

Magical Correspondences of Some Plants

ALDER (*alnus glutinosa*)

corr. – bridges, diplomacy, harmony, music, oracles

- for spells to create a bridge between differing points of view, to settle disputes
- to strike the note of harmony in a relationship
- to invoke wise mediation or advice
- to increase oracular abilities (the singing voice that foretells fate)
- to invoke protection for the land
- to help a budding musician develop his/her talent

APPLE (*pyrus malus* and other species)

corr. – love, health, beauty, poetry, sexuality, magical and prophetic power, faery knowledge

- for love spells and divination concerning love
- for the awakening of psychic, magical and creative abilities

- for healing physical illnesses and for rejuvenation
- for potency and skill as a poet or prophet
- for making links with the faeries
- for spells to increase beauty as well as youthfulness

ASH (*fraximus excelsior*)

corr. – balance, justice, travel, healing, connection between worlds/factions/species, the web of life

- for magic to heal any kind of rift between lovers or even between, say, logic and intuition within oneself, to restore correct balance
- for spells of justice
- to come into harmony with fate and fulfil the best posible destiny
- for safe travel, within either the everyday world or the inner one (the witch's broom, traditionally, has an ash pole for a handle, as well as birch twigs and a willow binding)

BETONY (*stachys betonica*)

corr. – courage, healing, optimism

- for spells to relieve anxiety and even to help a person overcome their most terrible fears
- to heal someone of despair, uplifting their mood and restoring hope
- to increase mental clarity and to boost confidence and courage

BIRCH (*betula alba*)

corr. – purification, beginnings, beauty, learning, faery, love, fertility

- for spells of psychic protection and purification
- for new beginnings, free of malign influences
- for grace and beauty and freshness (Birch transforms anything crass or crude to a more refined and subtle state)
- for spells of self-development
- for inspiration, zest and energy
- for love and fertility
- to increase awareness of faery presences

BLACKBERRY (*rubus fruticosa*)

corr. – sacrifice, transformation

- for magic that sacrifices your ego or personal interests to a greater principle
- for giving up something such as an addiction or bad habit and replacing it with a healthier pattern or creative endeavour

BUTTERCUP (*ranunculus bulbosus*)

corr. – wealth, gold

- for spells to gain prosperity or inner riches (or both)
- for magic that increases your sense of your personal worth

CELANDINE (*chelidonum majus*)

corr. – clear sight

- for spells to develop clairvoyance
- to counter the effects of misinformation by bringing clarity
- to see the way out of an imprisoning situation

DANDELION (*taxacum officinale*)

corr. – cleansing, relaxation, communication, the art of timing

- for spells of emotional or physical healing, especially in complaints which require a cleansing or unclogging process
- for magic to make things 'come out', e.g. to bring out the truth of a matter, or to move things on or out if some area of your life has stagnated
- to bring a time of relaxation in which to deal with an emotional backlog and so work through problems
- to increase psychic ability
- to communicate with distant friends or with spirits

ELDER (*sambucus nigra*)

corr. – healing, death and rebirth, contacting the dead

- for wise guidance or help through a time of loss or serious crisis
- to gain understanding about the afterlife and reincarnation
- to help in psychic communication with the dead
- for spells of healing
- for rites to bring a new start or a rebirth of something, following a loss, an illness or any big life change
- to help see the faeries (it is said that spending the night in an elder grove is one way to do this)

ELM (*elmus campestris*)

corr. – the land, agriculture, the past

- for spells to reconnect with old, lost knowledge about how to be at one with the land, especially in respect of agriculture (in the British landscape, mature elms are now a memory, a gentle haunting, bound up with folk-lore and poetry and with the recollections of older people)

- to bridge the worlds of past and present and so invoke a revival of cultural or spiritual heritage
- for magic to help bring environmental harmony

Note: elms are not extinct; it is just that, following Dutch Elm disease, there are only small ones now.

EYEBRIGHT (*euphrasia officinalis*)

corr. – clarity, joy, clairvoyance

- for spells to increase positivity and cheerfulness (to 'look on the bright side')
- to develop or strengthen clairvoyance
- to 'see the light', to have a revelation about any matter which has been a source of confusion

FIR (Norway spruce – *picea abies*)

corr. – birth, gifts, motherhood, Winter Solstice, change, turning points

- for spells to bring something to birth, such as a new project or work of art
- for magic to help with safe childbirth
- for new insight, especially about your own gifts or talents
- for rites to bless and well-wish the newborn
- to invoke for increased generosity within the world

GORSE (*ulex europaeus*)

corr. – wealth, creativity, eggs, hares

- for spells to increase prosperity (or inner riches) while in a seemingly barren or weak position
- to bring good opportunities (or to become aware of those already there)
- to find or attract 'treasure', whether physical or spiritual
- to increase positivity, fertility or creativity

HAWTHORN (*crataegus oxyacantha*)

corr. – seclusion, hermitage, otherworldly fastness, faery realm, trials or ordeals undergone for love, commitment

- for rites of dedication to any form of work that requires some degree of solitude
- for spells to invoke a retreat, such as a lonely cottage in which to write a book – or simply a time free from interruption wherever you happen to be
- to invoke the aid of the faeries
- to attract a lover who shares your particular commitment
- to heal unbalanced sexuality
- to change destructive anger into positive assertion and constructive action

HAZEL (*corylus avellana*)

corr. – divination, poetry, wisdom, water, salmon

- for magic that helps you achieve knowledge, wisdom, eloquence or the gift of poetry
- for water divining
- to have wishes granted (in Wales, this was said to happen, if you wore a hazel twig hat)

HOLLY (*ilex aquefolium* or *tinne*)

corr. – protection, strength

- for spells to bring psychic or physical guardianship of a home, person, family, tradition, place, project etc.
- to grow beyond jealousy and spite or to protect yourself from their effects in others
- for the right use of assertiveness
- to gain spiritual strength

HONEYSUCKLE (*lanicera periclymenum*)

corr. – life cycles, double spiral, luck, sexuality

- for spells to help a person to flow with the cycles of life creatively – to let go of the past
- for luck and prosperity and for magic to help you know when to take a gamble
- to have the golden touch in business or other matters
- for women, to increase sexual energy

HOPS (*humulus lupulus*)

corr. – conviviality, luck, friendship, healing, peace, relaxation

- for spells to bring rest or heal a person of insomnia
- to bring cooperation within a group
- to draw good luck and friends to your home
- for magic to help you integrate with a new group or community
- to heal unbalanced instincts and (in women) increase passion

IVY (*hedera helix*)

corr. – sacrifice, change, intoxication, fidelity

- for magic to help with constructive sacrifice, such as giving up an addiction or giving time and energy to something worthwhile
- for spells to help with survival, through a hard time (since ivy remains green through the dark season of the year)
- for constancy and fidelity, in spite of difficult challenges
- for spells to bring a desired change, such as attitudes, lifestyle or consciousness

JUNIPER (*juniperis communis*)

corr. – psychic cleansing, exorcism, healing, justice

- for spells of psychic purification and for banishing negativity from the home
- to protect against ill-wishes and also to help banish the effects of an ill-wish that has already been made
- for gaining or restoring justice and for protection against injustice
- for expelling bad spirits, especially the kind that cause illness

MEADOWSWEET (*filipendula ulmaria*)

corr. – happiness, comfort, home, marriage

- for spells of peace, especially domestic harmony
- to strengthen and bless a marriage
- to invoke happiness and joy
- to ease pain

MISTLETOE (*viscum album*)

corr. – peace and goodwill, fertility, reconciliation

- to invoke love that suspends hostilities and restores peace and goodwill
- for magic to increase fertility and so to aid in conception (warning: the berries are poisonous)
- for inner fertility, resulting in new creative work
- to help bring reconciliation after a quarrel with a friend or lover, or to resolve conflicting impulses within yourself

NETTLES (*urtica urens/urtica dioica*)

corr. – power, transmutation, snakes, hex-breaking, the underworld, healing

- to help or heal during a time of emotional or spiritual 'descent'
- for spells to transmute a painful experience into a beneficial lesson or some kind of spur to personal growth
- to restore creative will, energy or power, following an ordeal
- to break an ill-wish

OAK (*quercus robur*)

corr. – strength, knowledge, protection, hospitality, luck, solid achievement, doorways

- for magic to increase physical, mental, emotional spiritual or psychic strength
- for spells to gain access to knowledge, particularly of magic or herbalism
- for male potency and fertility
- for spells to protect your home from robbers or any kind of attack, including of a psychic nature
- to draw in kindly visitors and to enlarge your circle of friends

- to bring good luck (carry an acorn as a charm)
- for magic to achieve impressive results from small beginnings ('great oaks from little acorns grow')

PRIMROSE (*primula vulgaris*)

corr· – poetry, pleasure, dalliance, immortality, beauty

- for spells to bring a time of playfulness, ease and enjoyment, therefore to drive out stress
- to bring happiness
- to increase beauty
- for creative inspiration, especially in poetry

RED CLOVER (*trifolium pratense*)

corr. – balance, luck, emotional healing, cleansing, protection

- for magic to bring the elements of the self into a new or improved balance
- to bring good fortune
- to attract money
- for psychic protection and psychic cleansing
- to heal depression, grief or bitterness

ROSE (*rosa* spp.)

corr. – love, beauty, compassion, heart

- to increase happiness in a love affair or marriage by boosting the physical passion and also deepening the emotional bond
- for spells to attract a lover
- for spells to soften your own or someone else's heart, increasing compassion and empathy

- to increase beauty, including inner beauty
- for emotional healing and to bring peace
- to heal damaged sexuality (in women) and to increase femininity and female sexual confidence

ROWAN (*sorbus aucuparia*)

corr. – protection, creativity, healing, familiar spirits, stakes (as in the 'staking' of vampires)

- for spells to bring success or good health and for laying to rest what haunts us, obstructing success or health
- to end any haunting, whether by a bad spirit or a recurring memory or to banish a situation that has become very draining (rowan combats vampirism – choose something to symbolize the bad spirit, memory or situation, then 'stake' it, piercing it straight through with a rowan twig)
- for psychic protection
- for creative inspiration
- for spells to help you achieve visionary states or to make a connection with a familiar spirit

STRAWBERRY (*fragaria vesca*)

corr. – treats, faeries, feasts, good fortune

- for magic to invoke happiness, good times, pleasure, the good things in life
- for spells to bring contact with kindly, helpful faeries. (Carrying a strawberry leaf is said to help with this)
- for good fortune

VALERIAN (*valeriana officinalis*)

corr. – relaxation, healing, peace, love

- for spells to heal trauma, shock or severe stress and to promote peace
- to help bring reconciliation after a quarrel
- to enhance a feeling of security and tranquility, within the home
- surprisingly, in view of its unpleasant smell, to attract a lover

VIOLET (*viola odorata*)

corr. – mysticism, love, romance, spirit realms

- for magic to help you achieve a more mystical, poetic love affair, state of consciousness or way of life
- to enable you to commune with faeries
- to increase awareness of beauty (helpful in spells which aim to develop people's appreciation of nature)
- to attract love

WILLOW (*salix* spp.)

corr. – mediums, witches, poets, mourning, healing, contacts with spirits, protection

- for spells to aid clairvoyance and all psychic abilities
- for protection (the old saying 'knock on wood' or 'touch wood' originally referred to knocking three times on a willow tree to avert evil)
- for magical power
- to heal unbearable anguish or any kind of pain and to overcome self-pity or resentment
- for the magic which transforms suffering into creativity, such as emotional loss into poetry or music
- to bring contact with spirits

YEW (*taxus baccata*)

corr. – resurrection, rebirth, contact with the dead

- to bring regeneration when all seems lost in a time of emotional, psychic or spiritual exhaustion
- to invoke the power of recovery, by which we return from crisis or illness into renewed strength or health
- to help bring any kind of rebirth, for example of hope or of a cherished relationship
- to assist in sending a psychic message to a lost loved one such as a dead parent, child, lover or friend

Bibliography

Aburrow, Yvonne, *Auguries and Omens: The Magical Lore of Birds* (Capall Bann, 1994)

Anderson, William, *Green Man: The Archetype of our Oneness with the Earth* (HarperCollins, 1990)

Beth, Rae, *Hedge Witch: A Guide to Solitary Witchcraft* (Hale, 1990)

Beth, Rae, *The Hedge Witch's Way: Magical Spirituality for the Lone Spellcaster* (Hale, 2001)

Cunningham, Scott, *Cunningham's Encyclopedia of Magical Herbs* (Llewellyn, 1985)

Cunningham, Scott, *Magical Aromatherapy* (Llewellyn, 1989)

Cunningham, Scott, *Cunningham's Encyclopedia of Crystal, Gem and Metal Magic* (Llewellyn, 1991)

Davis, Patricia, *Aromatherapy: An A-Z* (C.W. Daniel 1988)

Davis, Patricia, *Subtle Aromatherapy* (C.W. Daniel 1991)

Franklin, Anna, *Familiars: Animal Powers of Britain* (Capall Bann, 1997)

Lavendar, Susan & Franklin, Anna, *Herb Craft: A Guide to the Shamanic and Ritual Use of Herbs* (Capall Bann, 1996)

Glass-Koentop, Patalee, *The Magic in Stones* (Llewellyn, 1989)

Green, Marian, *Natural Magic* (Element Books, 1989)

Grieve, M., *A Modern Herbal* (Penguin Books, 1931)

Ingerman, Sandra, *Soul Retrieval* (Harper, San Fransico, 1991)

Matthews, Caitlin, *Singing the Soul Back Home* (Element Books, 1995)

McIntyre, Anne, *The Complete Floral Healer* (Gaia Books, 1996)

Mynne, Hugh, *The Faerie Way* (Llewellyn, 1996)

Paterson, Jacqueline Memory, *Tree Wisdom* (Thorsons, 1996)

Romani, Rosa, *Green Sprituality: Magic in the Midst of Life* (Green Magic, 2004)

Roney-Dougal, Serena, *Where Science and Magic Meet* (Vega, 2002)

Roney-Dougal, Serena, *The Faery Faith* (Green Magic, 2003)

Ryall· Rhiannon, *The Magic of Herbs* (Capall Bann, 1996)

Skelton, Robin, *The Practice of Witchcraft Today* (Hale, 1988)

Skelton, Robin, *Spellcraft: A Manual of Verbal Magic* (Routledge & Kegan Paul, 1978)

Stewart, R.J., *The Living World of Faery* (Mercury, 1995)

Valiente, Doreen, *Natural Magic* (Hale, 1975)

Rae Beth can be contacted through her website, www.raebeth.com
or via
Robert Hale Ltd
Clerkenwell House
Clerkenwell Green
London EC1R 0HT